PRAISE FOR *REC*

I am convinced that we must foster a way of being Christian that looks like Jesus of Nazareth, whose gospel way can be described as loving, liberating, and life giving. We are profoundly in need of just such a Jesus Movement in our time. Bishop Claude Payne's *Reclaiming Christianity* presents a proven model for congregations to use to make the loving, liberating, and life-giving way of Jesus a reality in and through them. Bishop Payne has been a significant mentor to me in my ministry as a bishop. This book will enable him to mentor clergy and lay leaders in the work of forming followers of Jesus Christ who truly bear witness to his way of love, in their lives and in the world.

Michael B. Curry
27th Presiding Bishop and Primate
The Episcopal Church

Reclaiming Christianity identifies why spirituality has been weakened for decades—and then shows how it can be effectively nurtured and shared. It also advocates mutual respect among Christians and all beyond, showing how the love that underlies the gospel and scripture can be utilized in a way to leaven society, even as it strengthens the church.

Richard Rohr OFM
Best-selling spiritual writer
Founder, Center for Action and Contemplation

Bishop Payne calls upon the church and each individual in the church to "reclaim" God's love story. Throughout his book, Bishop Payne presents different practical models, so every person will be enabled to participate in the Jesus Movement today.

John L. Peterson
Canon for Global Justice and Reconciliation,
Washington National Cathedral
Former Secretary General,
Worldwide Anglican Communion

One of the Episcopal Church's elder statesmen, Bishop Payne possesses the wisdom and perspective of a long ministry and projects the positive energy and optimism of youth. This practical book affirms the principles of good teaching and effective mission: engagement of the whole person, learning in community, sharing leadership, and (my favorite) reading the Bible together. True to his affirmation of the power of teams, Bishop Payne shares the voices of many peers and colleagues with whom he has ministered over the years. Readers will find ideas and suggestions in its pages, and between the lines, they will be moved by Claude Payne's faith, hope, and love.

Cynthia Briggs Kittredge
Dean and President,
Seminary of the Southwest

Reclaiming Christianity delivers practical spiritual guidance for church members and leaders who want their congregations to become more warm and welcoming, who want to see younger families visit and become dedicated members, and who want to feel the joy of authentic spiritual vitality. Bishop Payne has seen the eight guidelines in this book work in real life, and your congregation could be the next to experience the power of "un-privatizing your faith" and "spiritual transmission." A great resource for classes, vestries, and other leadership groups to discuss chapter by chapter.

Brian D. McLaren
Author, *The Great Spiritual Migration*

Bishop Payne has been a thought leader for more than twenty-five years. In *Reclaiming Christianity*, he brings that wisdom to bear on the art of formation. From his own spiritual journey to best practices by congregational leaders today, he challenges the church to deepen its collective sense of faith through spiritual growth and evangelism. Payne offers a road map to guide leaders and members of their congregations in crafting deeper relationships with God, the church, and one another as disciples.

C. Andrew Doyle
Author, *The Jesus Heist* and *Vocătiŏ*
Bishop, Episcopal Diocese of Texas

RECLAIMING
CHRISTIANITY

A Practical Model for Spiritual
Growth and Evangelism

Claude E. Payne

ISBN 978-0-880-28462-2

Forward
Movement
inspire disciples. empower evangelists.

RECLAIMING
CHRISTIANITY

A Practical Model for Spiritual Growth and Evangelism

Claude E. Payne

Forward Movement

Cincinnati, Ohio

TABLE OF CONTENTS

INTRODUCTION

Imagine a young, single mother of two struggling, wanting something better. She decides to "try" church. On Sunday morning she forces herself to get up, feed and dress the children, leave the house on time. She referees a squabble between the two as they proceed to their destination. She's anxious, not only about her overall situation but also about what will happen next, not knowing whether her expectations will be met. Only the deep desire for something better counters her multiple fears and anxieties.

When she and her children are met by ushers or greeters with a countenance that is warm, confident, and engaging, their positive demeanor lifts her spirits. They recognize her household as having importance and proceed to draw them into the community. Because of their welcome and affirmation, she begins to think that she is in a good place, for what she experiences is a love beyond what is spoken, the kind that touches the soul.

When we are in church, and in the presence of God, we are in a good place; we are in a place of welcome and of spiritual nurture. But why does the church not always feel like a place of spiritual nurture? What is the disconnect between what we know to be true about the church and what far too many experience? What I present in this book is a way to reconnect, a pathway to spiritual nurture that blossoms into something huge. It is not speculative but based on ministry already underway. After many years of ordained ministry, I have never been more optimistic about the future of Christianity. I find enormous energy, high levels of dedication, and a ready willingness among the faithful. I also find church members know intuitively that institutional conflict over divisive issues—gender and sexuality being the most pressing— prevents us from realizing the very things we most want from church: rich inner spiritual lives; a way to come together to minister to a highly conflicted world; connection with God or the Holy; and deeper connections with our neighbors.

A major thrust in *Reclaiming Christianity* is the strengthening of the spiritual. My own happy discovery is that many faithful and dedicated Christians are strong spiritually. They believe. They care. They work hard and give generously of themselves, their wealth, and their talents. They are repositories of enormous internal spiritual treasure. Yet there is a disconnect between the treasure and wisdom possessed by spiritually engaged Christians, and what many of us experience in Sunday morning worship. Spirituality among Christians is privatized, assumed, and kept under wraps, hidden, internalized, and essentially held in secret. Men and women are happy to talk with one another about personal situations in their families, to talk about deeply held political convictions and their fears about whatever their next life stage holds—but they are rarely comfortable talking about their intimate lives with God. People might, in the privacy of their own thoughts, identify the divine as the source of their spiritual lives—but we too often don't take the next step of exploring how the divine is manifested in our day-to-day lives or in events in our communities.

In these pages, I aim to help readers "unprivatize" their faith. I do this by presenting what I have found to be *an effective way of gospel transmission or spiritual transmission.* By "spiritual transmission" and "gospel transmission," I mean the transfer of spirituality—knowledge about, language for, and practices that help us connect with spirituality's source, power, and guidance— from one person to another. I present a model of Christian formation that can nurture those, like the young mother I just described, who come to church seeking a spiritual foundation, a foundation powerful and clear enough that they can readily begin transmitting it to their children. Equally significant, this model enables those leading the local church—lay and clergy— in a process of spiritual formation and spiritual transmission to enhance their already strong spiritual roots. The process I outline in this book affects every aspect of church life: enhancing vision, preaching, teaching, fellowship, study, outreach, and worship.

The model I present for spiritual transmission is intimately connected to the Bible. I offer a fresh look at Holy Scripture, interpreting it through the lens of love, just as Jesus himself did. Reading scripture as a love story between the divine and creation makes it possible for the Bible to unify Christians— Christians of different denominations and Christians at odds with one another within denominational boundaries. Reading scripture as a love story helps make room for an evangelism that is based on mutual respect for fellow Christians, all the while acknowledging divisive issues. This same mutual respect also acknowledges other religions without compromising gospel integrity. It gives to the faithful a far more comprehensive way to use scripture, especially those parts that are or seem to be harsh or confusing, at odds with what we know to be true, just, and loving.

Since retiring as bishop of the Episcopal Diocese of Texas in 2003, I have had the grand privilege of continuing ministry on both a local and denominational basis. Though my frame of reference is Episcopalian, what I present can be adapted for other Christians and Christian traditions. And although I write as a priest and bishop, I am writing for lay people as well as clergy. I think it is imperative that lay people join clergy in pursuit of this expanded view of the Christian faith. Indeed, any approach to spiritual transmission, any discussion of the mission of the church that neglects lay people and focuses overly on clergy is surely wrongheaded—and doomed!

I have included questions at the end of each chapter to prompt reflection and discussion about the continuing quest for recovery, renewal, and reclaiming. So, let us begin.

CHAPTER 1
RECLAIMING **SPIRITUALITY**

Where does spirituality come from? That's a theological question as much as it is a historical one, for to explore spirituality from the beginning point is to remember that humans have a spiritual birthright that comes from being made in the divine image. We are engaging spirituality when we experience something that touches the innermost part of a human existence, namely the soul. This spiritual encounter affirms life as of value, gives us an inner security that builds hope for all life, and opens the mind to the presence of something beyond, something that inspires.

Author and theologian Frederick Buechner, in his memoir *Telling Secrets*, describes what he calls "the deepest self":

> Life batters and shapes us in all sorts of ways before it's done, but those original selves which we were born with, and which I believe we continue in some measure to be no matter what, are selves which still echo with the holiness of their origin. I believe that what Genesis suggests is that this original self, with the print of God's

thumb still upon it, is the most essential part of who we are and is buried deep in all of us as a source of wisdom and strength and healing which we can draw upon or, with our terrible freedom, not draw upon as we choose.

Buechner is describing the soul, that part of a human that is the essence of one's being, in which spiritual treasure develops and is stored.

Rooted in each individual's soul, spirituality is lived out in our ordinary, workaday lives, and enacted through our beautiful and broken bodies. Connecting our inner longings, our existential stirrings, and the prayers of our soul to the mind, heart, ears, eyes, and feelings (our emotional or affective lives) is a part of spiritual formation. And, just as spirituality begins in the soul but is expressed through the body, so too it begins with the individual but grows as it becomes a working part of something larger, the church.

In recent times, one of the most inspiring, insightful examples of spiritual treasure comes from the actions and words of the relatives of the people slain inside the Emanuel African Methodist Episcopal Church in Charleston, South Carolina in June of 2015. *The Washington Post* and other media sources reported that at a bond hearing, the first public appearance of Dylann Roof, the twenty-one-year-old killer, the relatives offered him forgiveness and said they were praying for his soul. "I forgive you," said Nadine Collier, the daughter of seventy-year-old Ethel Lance, as her voice broke with emotion. "You took something very precious from me. I will never talk to her again. I will never, ever hold her again. But I forgive you. And have mercy on your soul." One by one other relatives stood to speak. "I acknowledge that I am very angry," said the sister of slain church member DePayne Middleton-Doctor. "But one thing that DePayne always enjoined in our family…is she taught me that we are the family that love built. We have no room for hating, so we have to forgive." The words Jesus spoke from the cross come to mind here: "Father, forgive them; for they do not know what they are doing" (Luke 23:34).

It takes spiritual power to make this kind of witness. The relatives' words of forgiveness reveal a resource that has been accumulated through the years, an inner repository that is constantly held in storage, a life-tool that is always available. Such a witness can be offered by a Christian on a spiritual life pilgrimage, by one who not only has accepted Christ but who has also experienced Christ over time and incorporated those experiences into a personal accumulation of spiritual wealth. And just as those words of forgiveness were the fruit of a long, communal journey of faith, they also can be the loam in which other people's spiritual journeys take root and grow. While I can't presume to know the texture of what those Mother Emanuel family members were experiencing, the witness I received from them is one of spiritual depth: they seemed to be relying upon their soul's health and depth to face a path that otherwise would be one of retained hatred, desire for revenge, and ongoing despair. Their ability to forgive—their soul's need to forgive—was one step toward healing for them. Their ability to forgive was a powerful sermon of sorts for all listeners.

As happens so frequently, this spiritual treasure wasn't on exhibit in church, but outside the church—in this case, in a courtroom. It wasn't spoken as a way to convert but as a healthy way of survival, through a public exposition of faith. In other words, the "sermon" uttered in those words of forgiveness was born, in some deep way, in the church, but was expressed out in the world. This is always the way of Christian spirituality—it moves between ecclesial spaces and secular spaces, between church space and world space.

Let me cite a personal example of spirituality rooted in the church but taking expression beyond the church's doors. There is no drama to it and it pales in comparison to the account of those family members at the bond hearing—and yet, so often our most abiding spiritual experiences occur in undramatic, even humdrum circumstances. The church I attended as a teenager had a tradition of delivering flowers to shut-ins following Easter services. The beautiful altar flowers would be rearranged into bouquets following the last Easter morning service. I was among several teenagers who would then deliver them. On more than one occasion when I arrived at a home, the widow or widower would open the door and smile upon seeing the flowers. And then, when I told the receiver the flowers were from the church, the person's whole countenance changed—eyes, face, stance— the whole disposition.

In hearing that the church was the source of the flowers, the dear person understood that she (or he) had been remembered and not forgotten. They were not separated and alone but a part of God's greater household and community of faith. They were not formerly worthy, dedicated, and faithful members now sidelined by age and infirmity. They were not bypassed or forgotten. Those flowers carried with them appreciation, love, inclusion, and celebration. The flowers became an outward and visible sign of something deep within that affirmed life—and specifically the Christian life—in all its beauty and power. I was a surrogate of Christ, an ambassador for what the divine wants for people who can no longer live as active a life as when younger. I represented the church, the faith and the divine presence, power and love. The encounter had a holiness, not that the words exchanged were anything beyond the usual pedestrian expressions, but because of the origin and circumstances of the occasion.

Through that exchange, our souls were fed. The recipient's soul was fed through this special remembrance on the holiest day of the Christian year, when other families gathered and were occupied with their own celebrations. My soul was fed because I had the chance to be a giver—and the chance to be recognized as one bearing Christ. I was a simple teenager, usually invisible in an adult world except among those of my extended family and my own friends. Yet I had been part of an exchange that significantly impacted the life of an older adult, simply because I had been commissioned and sent by my rector for this ministry.

I came to verbalize the depth of that experience only in years after it actually happened; as a teenage flower-deliverer, I had no words to explain, even to myself, the depth of what really transpired. Just the impact was there. Though I didn't know it then, what happened became a part of my spiritual treasure, my inner spiritual strength. Delivering those flowers has been a part of my identity as a Christian. It was a part of the remembered feeling when, some twelve years later, I came to realize Christ's call to Holy Orders, to ordained ministry. The treasure has been a part of me ever since the events occurred.

I didn't understand, at the time of my floral delivery, what had happened. Because I didn't understand that a deep spiritual transaction had occurred, I was not as spiritually strengthened as I could have been. I was unable to identify that what had occurred in that floral exchange was, really, an encounter with Christ. Because I didn't have language with which to make sense of the experience—because I didn't know to name it as a moment of holy exchange—the event was privatized and remained isolated within me, out of reach of even my inner vocabulary.

The experience was real and profound, but was truncated by my own inability to give shape in language to what had occurred.

When the church fails to name and interpret the holiness in our midst, we fail to nurture members at their most important point of need. My experience of delivering flowers as a teenager, and only later reflecting on and being able to see the deeper meaning of the experience, illustrates a pattern that I believe is fundamental to the Christian spiritual life: We grow spiritually through encounter followed by reflection. This pattern appears throughout scripture—consider the resurrection account from the Emmaus story (Luke 24:13-35). On an open road two men are joined by a third who opens scripture to them and explains how it reveals Jesus. Only after this man blesses and breaks the bread at a meal and then disappears do the remaining two realize that they have encountered the risen Lord. "Were not our hearts burning within us," they say to each other. Something profound had happened. It had been unpredictable beforehand, and there was no indication it could happen again. Yet it changed their lives. This is the nature of the spiritual. In occurs when the unexpected evolves in quite natural ways, and its importance is magnified afterward. For these two men the experience does not end in Emmaus. They return to Jerusalem to tell the disciples what has happened. They share their story, and in that sharing the souls of all hearers are fed. For these two men, it is the second feeding of the day.

To cite still another example, C. S. Lewis has been a source of inspiration for millions of Christians, all stemming from his conversion, his discovery of the soul. Andrea Monda, in her article "The Conversion Story of C. S. Lewis,"[i] says of him:

---

[i] Published in L'Osservatore Romano, Weekly Edition in English, July 16, 2008, 4

[His] intelligence was subtle, his curiosity boundless, his acumen amazing, his dialectic power exceptional; yet something came into play that shattered his seemingly firm belief in the inexistence of God, for in life there is always something else, something unforeseen, unnoticed, or surprising.

Monda quotes Lewis:

You must picture me alone in that room at Magdalen, night after night, feeling, whenever my mind lifted even for a second from my work, the steady, unrelenting approach of Him whom I so earnestly desired not to meet. That which I greatly feared had at last come upon me. In the Trinity Term of 1929 I gave in, and admitted that God was God, and knelt and prayed: perhaps, that night, the most dejected and reluctant convert in all England.

Lewis was touched by the divine, and was able to "admit"— that is, reflect on—what had happened; thus he claimed his spiritual birthright.

Spiritual encounter followed by deepening spiritual understanding is a fundamental pattern of the Christian life. And it is a fundamental call of the church to be a place where people can share in that pattern together. Preaching, teaching, praying, serving community needs, and advocating for justice are tools to help people identify their spiritual experiences and to put into practice what spirituality directs. Like a seed that needs soil, water, and light, spirituality grows best as it is shared with others within the community of faith, simultaneously nurturing the speaker and those who hear.

My wife and I have a back porch that faces the rising sun. Since there is a vacant field immediately to the east, we can watch the rays of the almost visible sun reflect on low-lying clouds, all of which make a beautiful sunrise. What actually happens, as the sunlight illumines clouds, creates such a moving scene—some mornings, it practically defies speech. Yet this kind of sight displays a beautiful majesty that points to something more than sunlight hitting particles of moisture in the air. It points to the divine. This recognition reflects a prayer from the Episcopal *Book of Common Prayer*: "Open, O Lord, the eyes of all people to behold thy gracious hand in all thy works, that rejoicing in thy whole creation, they may honor thee with their substance, and be faithful stewards of thy bounty" (329). But if people only see a beautiful sunrise, and not a revelation of its divine source, their lives and their potential spiritual wealth are diminished. It is my fervent prayer that this book will help the church help people see all the sunsets for what they are—testimony to their Maker; sermons of praise to the Creator and Redeemer of all.

DEVELOPING SPIRITUAL TREASURE

Over the many centuries of its history, the church has developed practices of spiritual nurture and spiritual transmission. Here I'll look at several practices, already flourishing in many churches, that very effectively help people develop their spiritual treasure: Bible study, spiritual direction, faith-sharing venues, and renewal ministries of various types.

Most foundationally, the spiritual is nurtured through Bible study. In small-group Bible study, participants are fed not only by their encounter with scripture but also by the opportunity to connect with other people. Bible study, then, works on two levels, immersing participants in God's revelation to the church and giving people a chance to know—and love—their neighbors. The same can be said for study and prayer groups. Participants focus not only on what they seek to understand but also develop bonds of affection, faith, mutual concern, and support for themselves—and often for many beyond. They share spiritual experience and build spiritual treasure.

The rise in the practice of spiritual direction is another effort to nurture the soul and feed spiritual hunger. As Liz Budd Ellmann, former executive director of Spiritual Directors International, writes on that organization's website, "Spiritual direction explores a deeper relationship with the spiritual aspect of being human. Simply put, spiritual direction is helping people tell their sacred stories every day." Spiritual direction offers a means to address people's spiritual hunger on a personal one-by-one basis, and it can be especially useful when people feel there is something missing from their spiritual lives

Ellman continues:

> Spiritual direction has emerged in many contexts using language specific to particular cultural and spiritual traditions. Describing spiritual direction requires putting words to a process of fostering a transcendent experience that lies beyond all names, and yet the experience longs to be articulated and made concrete in everyday living. It is easier to describe what spiritual direction does than what spiritual direction is. Our role is not to define spiritual direction, but to describe the experience.

It's important to underscore that spiritual direction is built upon individuals' spiritual treasures. It helps individuals understand, appreciate, and use the treasure already within them in the building of a holier and fruitful life.

Another practice that can help foster a deeper, more articulate spirituality is Sharing Faith dinners, which are becoming more popular in several Episcopal dioceses. They are fashioned after Houston Interfaith Ministries' Amazing Faith Dinner Dialogues, which began in 2007. Then mayor Bill White wanted to discover ways to promote dialogue and education across ethnic and religiously diverse segments of the population. The Interfaith Conference of Greater Milwaukee began a similar effort in 2013. Carol Barnwell, director of communication for the Episcopal Diocese of Texas, spearheaded the adoption of this model for church use in 2012 and invited other dioceses to join in the effort. "It's funny that we have to plan an evening to talk to friends about our faith, but each time I've done Sharing Faith, it's been a gift," says Barnwell. "To enjoy the hospitality of people I may not know is always lovely. And to hear the very personal experiences of God from others is a humbling experience. Each time, I feel like I've received a gift, and each story allows me to see God in a new way."

Telling spiritual stories—stories of living encounter with the Living God—is vital for the spiritual life. The principle aim of such storytelling is not to convert hearers. Instead, the story is an occasion to express gratitude for the divine as it relates to humans in their struggles and ambitions. There is a humility in the process. Precious, life-lifting, powerfully insightful and therefore very personal stories are given air time. In the ordinary hustle and bustle of life, most people are reluctant to reveal this much of their inner life. There is little place to share something so highly personal. Thus, if these stories are not shared, the spirituality that undergirds them remains submerged.

Renewal movements also provide an avenue of spiritual nurture. Cursillo, a method developed by Roman Catholics and now used by many denominations, gathers people for four days in a setting where lectures are interspersed with conversation among participants. When I attended years ago, I found it very powerful. A similar renewal movement in the Episcopal Church is Faith Alive, a kind of lay witness ministry where a team is developed from Christians outside a congregation who come for a weekend to share stories of faith with parishioners. It too is very powerful, giving enormous energy to congregations in the afterglow of the weekend. Happening, designed for youth, is similar in scope. Still another renewal movement is Alpha, developed by Holy Trinity Brompton, a Church of England parish in London. It too is communal, utilizes faith-sharing stories, and has had broad ecumenical use worldwide.

So God continues to work in and for the church and, of course, God continues to work beyond the church. For instance, a well-known and highly respected non-church ministry that is built upon the spiritual is Alcoholics Anonymous. AA embraces reliance on a "higher power." Not incidentally, its centerpiece is the sharing of faith stories. AA thus confirms that God works everywhere and honors those who turn to the divine, regardless of whether they are churched. We Christians can celebrate the ongoing work and presence of God that occur beyond the church and help others come to see God's work around them.

There are delightful stories of how God works on those who have given up on their Christian identity. One example that moves me is the story of the late Harley Swiggum. In the course of World War II Swiggum was a part of the American military effort in the Pacific. He found himself stationed on Saipan as the front line of conflict moved onward. He had nothing to read in

English except a Bible. So even though he had dropped out of church, Swiggum started reading.

What he encountered was completely at odds with what he had experienced in the church of his childhood. In scripture he experienced a spiritual awakening and way of life that was not present in his early Christian upbringing. As contrasted to a church culture highly centered on the do's and don't's of life, through scripture he found a liberating spirituality articulated in scripture that led him into a life of inner strength and a calling to bless others through what he himself had received. Inspired by what he found in scripture, Swiggum came to an adult faith and was later ordained in the Lutheran tradition. In a desire to make scripture more readily available to people, he authored the Bethel Bible Series, which became a huge ecumenical tool for the study of God's Word.

Another story of the divine working in the lives of those beyond the church comes from the life of Phillip Jackson. He grew up in Chicago in a family that was nominally Unitarian. Phillip went to Amherst for his undergraduate degree and earned a law degree from Yale. Guaranteed a position in a major Chicago law firm, he exercised an option of waiting a year to begin work, with the only stipulation of employment being that he pass the bar exam. In his own words, he decided to go to Hawaii to "chill out" in the aftermath of years in school.

Arriving in Hawaii, he enjoyed it so much that he wanted to stay. Looking for work, he joined a small firm of five attorneys. He enjoyed the partners and liked the work, except that after three years he felt something was missing in his life. He reasoned that his job was essentially helping people either make money or keep it, or both. Then came the nagging question to himself, "Can I do this for the next thirty years"? Enter angst. Then came an inner voice saying, "You need to go to church." Since Phillip had a childhood connection to the Unitarian Church, he went there, but did not find anything that made him want to return. The next week while stopped at a traffic light, he noticed a church on the corner and heard an inner voice, "Go there." Reading the service time, he decided to follow the prompting.

Attending St. Clement's Episcopal Church the next Sunday, he discovered "a language that he had always known and could perfectly understand but couldn't explain why." It was the language of faith, for which his soul was hungry, and he liked it. Sunday by Sunday he took a back row pew until one Sunday the priest asked, "Who are you and what are you doing here?" Thus began a series of lunches between them, leading Phillip finally to say, "I don't think I can practice law for the rest of my life." The priest then said to him, "You are going to be a priest." Phillip recognized that he had been introduced to a vocation that matched his soul's need.

From there he was mentored by a family with three children and given John Stott's *Basic Christianity* to read. This led him to the response, "Lord, I give myself to you." This acknowledgment and acceptance of his conversion led next to his baptism. A week later his rector took him to see the bishop about the possibility of becoming a priest. The bishop told him to work for two years as a new Christian and return to talk again.

One evening some six weeks later Phillip prayed, "Lord, tell me what you want, and I'll do it." The next day, quite unexpectedly, the bishop called and wanted to see him again. At that meeting, the bishop said, "I've changed my mind. I want you to go to seminary this fall." Thus began a new trajectory that led to ordination and a life filled with the joy of ministry in an ordained capacity. Phillip now serves as vicar of Trinity Church, Wall Street, in New York

City. He is a priest because a divine call came to him completely outside any Christian church. He has experienced encounter after encounter since hearing the voice directing him to go to church. His story is testimony to the unlimited reach of Christ's action outside the church as well as within. Phillip has spiritual treasure, and it grows every time he tells his story of faith. And every time he tells his story, reminding listeners that the divine call can come to anyone at any time.

At the General Convention in 2015, the Rt. Rev. Michael B. Curry, then bishop of North Carolina, was elected presiding bishop for the entire Episcopal Church. His consistent and passionate focus has been to challenge the Episcopal Church to become a part of the Jesus Movement. The thrust of this movement is to place energy and attention into bringing what the church says and does more in line with what Jesus said and did. Bishop Curry defines the Jesus Movement as "following Jesus into loving, liberating, and life-giving relationships with God, with each other, and with the earth," and he calls upon Episcopalians to be evangelists, reconcilers, and conveners for conversation. This is a tremendously hopeful sign for Episcopalians and is already inspiring movement toward renewal in all its dimensions.

The initiatives described in this chapter, and many more not mentioned, indicate a slow but very sure and hopeful shift toward the renewal of Christianity in the church and in the world.

STRENGTHENING SPIRITUAL TRANSMISSION

The call of God—the eruption of the holy—may come in an epiphany, alone on a solitary walk, or in private, inner wrestlings. It may occur in conversation with another or others. But if there is only a solitary aspect to the relationship of any one believer and God, then spirituality and the spiritual treasure it creates is not nurtured well. Christian spirituality, operating on the grounds of a God who lives fundamentally in community with God's own self, by definition should not remain private. The spiritual is akin to love; it exists in the context of contact with others. It grows with continued contact. Spirituality is about heart and soul, about feelings and perceptions. It is about encounter, not information. Theology is not a source of the spiritual but rather the means of pointing to its reality, explaining it after the fact.

Thus, the church desperately needs a model of gospel transmission that honors the loam of solitude in which much spirituality originally roots but also recognizes the fundamentally communal and relational nature of spirituality. Furthermore, the church needs to cultivate practices of transmission that are keyed to fruitfulness and nurture in addition to productivity and success. At present our entire culture, secular and sacred, considers education as the way to address human needs and to create a productive society. It has been so supremely effective that modern society in Western countries has become highly skilled through all kinds of technological breakthroughs. People continue to be impressed and even awed by countless successes. As a society, people are a living legacy of the supremacy of the rational that the philosopher René Descartes put forth in his famous dictum, "I think and therefore I am." Carried to its conclusion, this precept elevates the mind and the rational to the exclusion of all else—to the exclusion of prayer, spiritual practice, and acts of faith and service. Existential rumination and nurture of the soul have been sidelined by modern secular society. But existential rumination and nurture of the soul are specialties of the church.

Consequently the field is wide open for Christians to implement a model of individual development by rooting it in what ordinary education does not furnish, namely those ties that bind people together, including the spiritual. Like love, spirituality is transmitted primarily by relationship. There are practical, even utilitarian, reasons for Christians to care about spiritual transmission. Spirituality is the church's greatest working and mission resource. So the very future of Christianity necessitates strengthening this singularly precious asset. Furthermore, in order to be more humane and just, society needs a stronger spiritual element. But there is an even deeper reason for the church to pursue a robust and organic practice of spiritual growth and spiritual transmission: The spiritual life is what we were made for. In other words, for the church to pursue "institutional survival" without pursuing spiritual vigor is wrong-headed in two ways at once. It's impossible, since the very thing that can make the church grow is spiritual vitality; and even if it were possible, it would be the tail wagging the dog, since the church exists not because God wants an institution but because God wants a cradle of spiritual nurture.

Thus, Christian formation must provide a way to pursue the sharing of faith stories, spiritual disciplines, and the integration of gospel content with faith experience at the heart of congregational life. I adopted such an approach to Christian formation years ago as rector of St. Martin's Episcopal Church in Houston. I recruited a team of lay people and trained them to be mentors for newcomers to the church in Inquirers' Classes. We gathered for discussion and study. Faith sharing at tables worked in tandem with lectures on the Christian faith, tying together experience and reflection upon the experience. The first element was providing a comfortable, safe place for conversation. This included time for getting acquainted with each other, and verbal assurance that there would be no element of judgment that would create a "me versus you" hierarchy in relationships. This established trust, the necessary springboard from which in-depth sharing could take place. At the conclusion of these sessions, newcomers so inclined were baptized or took vows of renewal. Each year, the mentors told me they had never experienced anything more spiritually rewarding in church.

The beauty and power of this model resides, in large measure, in peer learning and sharing among newcomers who are led by more seasoned members of the church. As they share stories of faith and personal spiritual practices, newcomers (and, indeed, also seasoned church members) are led to examine their own lives through the experiences of others. In that process they become inspired. At the same time they begin a bonding process with each other that counters the isolation so many feel, exemplified by the expression "alone in a crowd."

Nothing feeds my soul or adds to my own spiritual treasure more than being part of such a ministry. It gives me so much confidence that I no longer grieve about the marginalization of religion in secular culture. The recovery of a vital, attractive Christianity undergirded by increased spiritual energy is precisely what modern culture needs; the possibility that this straightforward ministry of Christian sharing and edification gives me a happy thrill and a hopeful heart.

FINAL THOUGHTS

It's a wonderful and fearful responsibility Christians have—the responsibility to enable other people to discover their own spiritual birthright and the existence of their souls. The aim of this book is to inspire members of our churches to act from a posture of confidence—and not from a posture of fear of decline —asking, "Is my church doing all it can to offer the treasures of Christianity to a world in need of spiritual nurture? And is my church doing all it can to help burnish the spiritual treasure already in our midst?"

REFLECT AND RESPOND

- In what ways do you identify with spiritual treasure?

- Is the concept of spiritual treasure attractive to you?

- How does spiritual transformation take place in your congregation?

- In what ways do you share your own spirituality or encounters with the divine, and with whom?

- How is your spirituality nurtured? When alone? With others?

- What is your definition of the soul and how is it tied to spirituality?

- How do you explain the increase of people who identify with no religion, or who claim to be spiritual but not religious? Are you or your congregation doing anything to address this? Is it ever a topic of discussion?

CHAPTER 2
RECLAIMING **CHRISTIAN FORMATION**

This chapter will take you deeper into the Christian formation model I developed that fosters the transmission of spirituality by using peer engagement—that is, Christians, both lay and clergy, sharing their spirituality and its roots with newcomers and faith seekers. The beauty of this model is that it begins with the soul, the image of God that is the birthright of all people. It focuses on the sharing of spiritual treasure in a setting that enables newcomers to contribute and engage. Those who share and those who listen are peers, fellow seekers endeavoring to grow. In a sense, each person is a leader of the group, because at varying points, each person speaks or "holds the floor." Each person asks questions when moved to do so. When newcomers discover that what they are hearing in Christian formation engages the truth that is already within them, faith is caught.

This is not indoctrination where one party is trying to persuade another. Instead it centers on an approach of humility, offered in love, and offered in support of what the others desire without any effort of trying to convince.

THE VISION

In the 1990s, I began to develop a team-based model for Christian formation. Built upon the affirmation of the soul as one's spiritual birthright, the model enables newcomers to identify, to nurture, and then to use spiritual treasure as a life guide and resource. The model unfolds around two nodes: 1) peer interaction between newcomers and trained table mentors; and 2) presentations that show how Christianity beautifully and powerfully frames, illumines, and interprets human experience. This formation model helps new church members prepare to be blessed to live a Christian life for personal well-being and to contribute to the development of a stronger society—so it includes consideration of Christian responsibility for self, church, and society, people's vision for their own personal ministry, and the centrality of faith to one's pilgrimage through life and into eternity.

This model draws on the best wisdom of contemporary pedagogy but turns those pedagogical practices to the spiritual by enabling newcomers to recognize and nurture their divinely given souls and then using their minds to identify a divine element in their experience of living. Hence, newcomers to the church are exposed to a fuller vision of reality. But newcomers are not the only people whose spiritual lives are engaged by this curriculum. An equally important part of this is additional spiritual nurture for the longer-term church members who serve as table mentors, guiding the group discussions that are central to the curriculum. This process is a means of highly effective gospel transmission that benefits all: clergy and laity; newcomers and long-time members; the intimate church community; and the world beyond the church's doors.

STRUCTURE AND SETTING

The model is currently being used at the Episcopal Church of the Heavenly Rest in Abilene, Texas. There, parishioners and clergy have introduced peer engagement and team methodology into a structure of weekly meetings with newcomers gathering at tables, each under the direction of a lay leader. After initial table conversation, a lecturer gives a talk about some dimension of basic Christianity. That specific subject exposes how theology built upon recognition and nurture of the soul opens the human possibility for spiritual power and divine guidance to build life through the accumulation of spiritual treasure. This conversation is followed by additional sharing about the lecture content and its personal impact. The aim is for newcomers to "catch" Christianity from other Christians while simultaneously developing a theological rationale for what they experience. As the series schedule draws to a close, participants find they are well prepared for Christian initiation through baptism or renewal of baptismal vows.

Describing his experience of Christian formation and what led to it, Stephen Weathers, who took the classes at the Church of the Heavenly Rest, has written a reflection he calls "My Journey:"

> My journey into the Episcopal Church was marked both by mysticism, for want of a better term, and by rationalism. Odd, perhaps, but it began with a radio program, accidentally encountered and unintentionally audited. A BBC shortwave broadcast of an Anglican liturgy—a form of worship of which, at the time, I was wholly ignorant—evoked an intense longing within me. A spiritual void was revealed. I found myself emotionally moved in ways totally out of keeping with my low-church upbringing. I couldn't account for such a

response. It was a somewhat mystical call, I realized only in retrospect, but I successfully ignored it for several decades. Later—much later—when, as an English professor, I on a whim included Richard Hooker in the syllabus for one of my courses, I discovered the rational grounds of Anglican theology. At every point—and this despite a rigorously biblical upbringing—I found myself concurring with Hooker. The encomium "judicious," so often applied to this Elizabethan theologian, I came to see as entirely warranted. I was struck by his unfaltering balance and remain so.

In time, these experiences coalesced, prompting my search for an ecclesiastical embodiment authentic to both my mystical call and my rational convictions. The result? I one day visited an Episcopal service and found some internal homing instinct activated. I sensed I was moving in the right direction. I had in the past been guilty, I confess, of having stereotyped Episcopalians as reserved, unemotional, and chilly specimens of the Christian faith. My experience, however, as I became better acquainted, refuted this stereotype at every turn. I couldn't have been more mistaken. Throughout the process leading up to my reception into the church, I met warm, demonstrative, and, at times, winsomely effusive believers. And now, thank God, I number myself among them.

Central to my decision was the influence of the New Member Formation Class I had begun attending. Each week, in a relaxed, convivial atmosphere, we inquirers were invited to explore open-ended discussion questions of deep spiritual import. Without exception, these well-designed interrogatives elicited conversation—conversation that quickly left superficiality behind and probed the soul's mysteries. Heart spoke to heart, deep to deep. Pain found commiseration. Confusion met with comfort. Facilitating the discussion at each table was an appointed church member who was endowed, it became clear, with the twin gifts of empathy and hospitality. I once remarked to our small-group facilitator that it was kind of her to devote time to us, a group of outsiders. "Oh, but you're not outsiders," she quickly assured me. "You're already a part of us." Such warm sentiments, expressed often in these contexts, did much to communicate the hospitable spirit pervading the church. Scheduled speakers joined us each week, moreover, to discourse on specific topics, inducting us deeper into the Christian faith and orienting us within an Episcopalian context. By the conclusion of the series, my mind was made up: I was, indeed, home.

This reflection is a testimony to the power and comprehensiveness of a formation model that unfolds around peer engagement, combining spiritual encounter with the rational.

The classes that are the heart of this formation ministry are acts of love—that is the most important thing to say about them, more important than any of the specific details about a given class session. God loves. Christ came to love. Christians are called to love. Classes are offered in and through love because newcomers will not feel the love of God if they don't first feel the love of their class leaders. The team—by their body language, eye contact, graciousness, and eagerness to listen—augment the intellectual content of Christianity. The warmth, anticipation of newcomers' needs, and preparation depth from the formation team translate in verbal as well as nonverbal ways to those who come.

Formation team leaders understand that they are there to offer an opportunity for newcomers to recognize and develop their individual spiritual treasure. This treasure comes from Christ, whether newcomers recognize it or not. Each person has a soul and spiritual identity. Consequently the formation task is to identify this part of human existence, lay claim to it, and enable individuals to build upon it as a way to a fuller and richer life. Existence of the soul attracted people to Jesus. Humans have an innate curiosity for exploration. A formation time designed to help people better understand themselves and utilize that knowledge to get more out of life is enormously attractive.

Remembering the familiar passage that reads, "Glory to God whose power, working in us, can do infinitely more than we can ask or imagine" (Ephesians 3:20), it is the sharing of such "power working in us" occasions that shape Christians and build spiritual treasure. Christians should be able to talk about these occasions, though, too often, we are in fact ill-prepared to discuss spirituality. In our society, huge human effort goes into development of the mind. Why not also for the soul? When newcomers grow in spiritual treasure, they are eager to accept Christ, join the church, take up the Christian pilgrimage through life, and offer themselves and what they have toward the church's mission.

How, then, does this formation model work, on the ground?

Prior to the start of the formation classes, invitations are sent to those expressing interest. The invitation list is composed of those who have had some contact with the church, whether at worship or otherwise, and who have expressed interest in learning more.

Letters, emails, telephone calls, and well-coordinated personal contact let newcomers know about the classes. Newcomers are told that they are under no obligation to join the church because of their participation.

Ideally, the model includes at least fifteen 75-minute sessions (fifteen minutes to gather, an hour for class time) scheduled for Sunday mornings. But the exact number of classes, the class time, and the content completely depend on local option. Heavenly Rest chose this schedule because it fits nicely between their two Sunday morning times of worship. Their sessions begin with a fifteen-minute assembly time in which participants put on name tags, get coffee, and are offered a small take-plate-to-table breakfast. The first formal fifteen minutes of class are given to table conversation around a question introduced by the table leader. Newcomers thus become better connected with other newcomers and with members of the formation team, who become their Christian guides. The next thirty minutes are for a lecture in which the speaker not only talks about Christian heritage and doctrine but also how they influence his or her personal life. Then comes another fifteen minutes of sharing.

The fifteen-week outline and the one-hour class duration is not written in stone. The classes can be offered at any time, such as a weekday evening. In larger congregations, classes can be offered in duplicate, such as on a Sunday morning with the same class offered again on a weekday evening. The program does not have to be offered on Sunday at all if another time is better for the community. Each congregation should modify the fundamentals of the base model to fit the local situation. The means of engagement and overall gospel transmission are the essentials. They can slowly build a renewed church culture that in time will lift the entire congregation.

Since the perfect attendance of newcomers is an ideal hardly ever realized, having sessions that last over a longer period enable participants to come and go on occasions when they cannot make a class. The overarching class goal is to integrate newcomers into the local church community, the body of Christ. There is no rush. While preparation for membership for those desiring it is the announced class goal, the deeper class goal is integration into the Christian faith in ways that lead to an individual's continued personal growth. Overall concern should be focused on preparing these newcomers for life after baptism as contrasted to merely getting them initiated.

A series like this is a challenge for clergy because of perceived time constraints. But once in place, the curriculum proves not burdensome but liberating. Shared leadership is essential, in part because it lessens the burden on any one clergy person. With a whole team working as a team, the entire endeavor functions like any ongoing class that has shared leadership. True, developing, recruiting, training, and commissioning team members take time. So does keeping up with the team after classes begin. But the time invested in creating a formation process is the most potent, energizing, and effective ministry endeavor I have ever experienced as a member of the clergy.

Further, clergy and lay colleagues build a team that allows all to flourish. Lay colleagues take on responsibilities that will expand ministry in every direction. And as a result, clergy end up doing those things they are best equipped to do, that rely on their seminary preparation. This type of Christian formation empowers and encourages laity to identify and deploy their own spiritual treasure. It also enhances clergy preaching, breaks their feelings of isolation, nurtures their own spirituality, and makes them far more effective and personally fulfilled. This happens because the preacher's experience of becoming a closer part of lives being transformed builds more confidence.

The course is open to all—newcomers, lapsed, those with no religious background, the curious, prospective new Episcopal Church members, and existing parishioners. It is a "come and explore" opportunity. Its aims are to:

♦ Help all newcomers discover and grow in their spiritual birthrights as children of God because each is made in the divine image, possessing a soul for the development of personal spiritual treasure.

♦ Challenge all to use that spiritual base to live more productive lives, to find ways of serving others in their needs, and to work in concert with all who aspire to promote a more just and loving society.

♦ Encourage weekly worship to coordinate class and worship experience. For many, this leads to membership in the Episcopal Church through baptism or the renewal of baptismal vows.

THE CLASSES

In order to give a more comprehensive overview of the course, here is a detailed description of the first several classes.

The first session is primarily devoted to creating an atmosphere of trust and welcome. At Heavenly Rest, shortly before class begins, a team of lay leaders gathers, prepared to greet newcomers and assist them in filling out name tags. As newcomers arrive, they are offered coffee and/or a small breakfast and are invited to sit at one of the tables. Lay leaders are already there, seated at each table. They introduce themselves, point out restroom locations, and begin conversation. As other attendees enter they move to tables and participate in the introduction process.

At the stated beginning time, a bell is rung and the lay leader calls the group to order and begins the session with a prayer. This person then self-identifies as a table leader and shares something of his or her sojourn at the church. That goes something like, "I'm Sue Smith, and I've been a member here since 2010. I became an Episcopalian in 2006 in Denver, Colorado, and was raised in a non-denominational church. I was attracted to the Episcopal Church by its liturgy, reverence, ability to adapt to changing times, and the friendliness of its people." The leader then asks another person to do likewise and reveal something personal along the same lines. One may say, "I'm _____, I have lived in (name of place) ten years and was invited to church a year ago by a friend and colleague from work. I have a Christian background but haven't been active in church since I was a teenager. I haven't been really looking for a church, but when invited, I decided to come see what it is like." All around the table, participants have an opportunity at self-introduction in this way.

After fifteen minutes, the rector, pastor, or designated leader begins the lecture part. The lecturer thanks everyone for coming and compliments their desire to explore Christianity in the Episcopal Church. The speaker then goes over the entire church schedule, as weekly attendance at worship is recommended to deepen the class experience (and is expected of those who are considering church membership)..The lecturer also explains that the classes are designed for spiritual development that *may* lead to church membership but emphasizes that no attendee is under any obligation to join the church. Thus newcomers are prepared for baptism or renewal of baptismal vows, but they understand that it is okay if they simply gain information about the Episcopal expression of Christianity and choose not to be baptized or sacramentally reaffirmed in their faith at the end of the course.

Each week, participants gather at tables—each week they can select the table of their choice—to focus on a specific question often related to the topic presented during the lecture period of the class. On this first day, the lecturer gives an overview of basic Christianity. A maximum of thirty minutes is taken for this, followed by another fifteen minutes of table conversation. The underlying purpose of this first session is to put newcomers at ease. Fellowship prevails. No obligation for church membership is pushed. All questions are encouraged. Anxieties are put to rest. Trust begins to build. The session ends with the table leader expressing appreciation for everyone's participation.

One of the most important aspects of this model is the blend of lecture and table discussion. Table discussion allows peer participation. Everyone gets to speak, ask, tell, or relate. They engage. Neither the mentors nor the presenters assume that, "We have something to share with you from which you will benefit." Rather the approach is, "We are interested in who you are, where you have come from, and what drew you to the Episcopal Church. We are ready to assist you to know more about us and our faith." Love is the motivating posture. Unspoken is that this format gives newcomers a forum to engage with church members for the duration of the classes.

This model gives newcomers a place to begin, develop, and grow in their faith. They interface in depth with clergy and lay leaders as the classes progress. The power of this is phenomenal. Newcomers are exposed to nonprofessional Christians. While clergy are expected to be spiritual and church leaders, the witness of laity who live out a gospel mandate is powerful beyond measure. Those newcomers who decide to be baptized or reaffirmed will have experienced living examples of what they can reasonably expect to live into.

The following week repeats the same format: newcomers are greeted, choose a table, get acquainted with anyone they haven't met, and move into table discussion after the leader's opening prayer. The question for the second week on the Heavenly Rest outline is about Christ: who is he (if anything) to each person at the table? Christ is foundational in Christianity. Spirituality comes from Christ. If later baptized or reaffirmed, class participants will be asked whether they accept Christ and are willing to follow him. So placing this emphasis at the outset sets a good reference from which to build everything else as the weeks unfold. Before asking for responses from newcomers, the leader begins by saying who Christ is to her or him. Most, even atheists, know something of Jesus. No one has to respond, but experience shows that most people will—newcomers who have made the effort to get to the classes are quite serious about matters of faith.

The lecture addresses the same question—emphasizing that Jesus comes to transform lives, something he has always done and still does. The rector usually gives this presentation and sets an overarching theological tone for the course. When I do this, I emphasize that for me Christ is spiritual power and guidance, the invisible divine power of the cosmos, who came to earth in the person of Jesus. Then and now he miraculously transforms lives and lifts them heavenward. Christ is the image of God, from whom Christians receive the divine identity. This opens a door to bring up the Holy Trinity, God made known through three different references. Though all analogies have their strengths, I find the three human ego states—parent, adult, and child, three "phenomenological realities" that operate in each person (described by Dr. Eric Berne, the founder of Transactional Analysis theory)—to be a helpful tool for thinking about the Trinity. Further, the Trinity introduces community, found in the Godhead, of which humans are an image. Life is communal, both internally, as in the three ego states, as well as externally with other persons. No one is created or continues to live solo. Thus, community defines both the Godhead and humanity. Then I share a story of faith to illustrate Christ as spiritual power and guidance for me, tying my experience to what I say about Christ.

After the lecture, there's a final fifteen minutes of table discussion about Christ's identity. Stories of faith are shared. These exchanges develop a life of their own. They become very rich and vibrant conversations because of the free-flowing process of peer engagement. They are the means by which the Holy Spirit enters the entire arena, moving those involved to deeper and deeper engagement with questions about faith.

Parenthetically, the practice of faith sharing is best done in such a structured setting. Renewal movements recognize this. People often do not feel comfortable sharing their stories in the usual routine of day-to-day conversation, or even at church. The intimacy of the table groups makes this kind of sharing a rich, authentic engagement, and enhances the catching of faith.

The third class is on the Bible. My approach—which I advocate in part because I believe it has the power to achieve Christian unity amidst diversity—is to view the Bible as a love story between God and creation. I am dedicated to this approach because it honors mutual respect that is a part of love. This trajectory provides a way to move beyond those readings of scripture now obsolete (i.e., reading biblical phrases like "the ends of the earth" to mean that the earth is flat) or compromised (i.e., wives being subject to husbands). Discussion focuses on how the participants think and feel about the Bible, how they were or were not taught as children to read the Bible, and how they experience the Bible today. Taken together, the lecture and the discussion give newcomers guidance on how they interpret the Bible as the Word of God.

The fourth class addresses the soul. Each person has a soul by birthright, made in the image of God and therefore having a spiritual component. Again, the table mentor tells a personal faith story, one that affected the soul and built spiritual treasure. The miraculous expectation aspect of Christianity is affirmed and encourages newcomers to think of times in their lives when the miraculous happened. That question—when did the miraculous occur in your life?—gives newcomers and table leaders alike a lens for reinterpreting their own life stories; the miraculous has always been present, but until you look through the lens of the miraculous, you won't know the miracles for what they are. These moments often become occasions when Christianity is "caught."

The session on *The Book of Common Prayer* is best scheduled to fit the Christian liturgical year. In the spring, schedule it before Lent, making Lent and Holy Week a vehicle for building the soul's health, enabling church life to complement class experience. Consequently, the Lenten focus of giving up something ties well with the human need to say "no" for maintaining health. It also reveals a motive for fasting. Ash Wednesday gains in significance and newcomers recognize how Christianity helps them make sense of life.

When the course is taught during the fall, other seasonal days can be explained. For instance, many Episcopal churches observe Saint Francis' Day on a Sunday around October 4, his feast day. The emphasis is on the environmental sacredness of creation. Those congregations having a blessing of pets explain that God is the creator and lover of all creatures, not just humans. An autumn course might also address All Saints' Day. (At all times of year, the course can explain the practice of saints' days and even digress into how the saints give a model for living a Christian life.)

Again, the entire class outline is appended to the end of this chapter, so I won't walk through each session in detail. But I'd be remiss if I didn't call attention to the class session on Holy Baptism (which Heavenly Rest covered in class eight). During this session, Episcopalians have special opportunity to expose the power and comprehensiveness of the Baptismal Covenant as a guide to Christian pilgrimage. The first part of the covenant is the Apostles' Creed. Then five questions are posed that outline how the covenant is to be kept.

The first question of the Baptismal Covenant is, "Will you continue in the apostles' teaching and fellowship, in the breaking of bread, and in the prayers?" This is derived from the communal nature of Christianity and compellingly lays out the necessity of regular corporate worship. Regular participation in both Holy Communion and private devotion sustain the faithful. They are reminders of personal spiritual treasure and the need to build upon it through connection to the body of the faithful. The second question is, "Will you persevere in resisting evil, and, whenever you fall into sin, repent and return to the Lord?" This question gets at a key piece of "personal spiritual hygiene," acknowledging human sin and the constant need to have its effects removed. The lecturer might make a special point of discussing the various ways of making confession, and at tables the mentors and newcomers share their own insights.

The third question is, "Will you proclaim by word and example the Good News of God in Christ?" Here, the discussion turns to spiritual outreach—to empowering each Christian to witness (verbally or nonverbally) in loving ways to spiritual treasure as a supreme source of life fulfillment and direction. This is evangelism, inviting others to share spiritual wealth. (More will be said about how to do this in Chapter 5, Reclaiming the Missionary Call.)

The fourth question is, "Will you seek and serve Christ in all persons, loving your neighbor as yourself?" The second part of the great commandment to love generates a vision of servanthood and the way the Christian is to behave toward others within the Church and to all beyond. It presents a Christ-like way to approach others, remembering the biblical exposition that the one who humbles self will be exalted.

The final question is, "Will you strive for justice and peace among all people, and respect the dignity of every human being?" Society is ever-changing, and some people have been left behind in every age. Regardless of political disposition, it's a Christian imperative to acknowledge the necessity to care for those who have been disenfranchised.

In the Baptismal Covenant, Episcopalian Christians have a comprehensive guide for growing spiritual treasure in their souls, all in pursuit of health in life. Other traditions can present their own way for the growing of Christian life. The result has beauty and power, offers hope, and follows in the tradition of Jesus. Essentially, these five questions of the Baptismal

Covenant point to the ways in which the covenant might be kept. The five say:

- Keep connected to the church

- Keep inwardly clean through confession

- Share spiritual treasure

- Keep humble and serve

- Strive for a just society

This class on baptism is one session where the table sharing schedule can be altered so that a brief lecture first introduces the five points of the Baptismal Covenant. Table discussion then centers on how each of the five points is observed. The final ten minutes can be used for someone from each table to share with the larger group something of special significance that was covered at his or her table.

The remaining classes unfold in much the same way. Any of them can be adapted in schedule, content, format, number of weeks offered, or otherwise. Each rector or lay person in charge has wide latitude to customize the classes for local needs, circumstances, and denominational focus. But I encourage adherence to the fundamentals of the curriculum—both the topics it covers and the blend of lecture and table conversation. This will foster personal contact among participants and team, integration of people through ideas and spiritual life, creative engagement of lay people and become a highly effective means for gospel transmission. Anyone utilizing this methodology should prepare for energizing and remarkable growth and personal renewal.

THE COMPLETE CLASS SCHEDULE

A draft schedule for the Church of the Heavenly Rest, including weekly subjects and table questions, follows. The sessions attempt to cover Christian basics so that the newcomer will have thorough grounding. In addition, those joining the church will have time to become acquainted in some depth with the mentors and hopefully with others in the congregation. Hence, by the end of the course, they will feel that they are a part of the church community, already launched on their pilgrimage.

BASIC CHRISTIANITY

Week One **(Suggest starting week of September 10)**

Welcome. Overview of Class and its vision of building spiritual treasure for those attending. Introduction of class leaders. Fielding questions. Getting acquainted.

Table discussion is about the class, addressing questions of participants.

Week Two

Jesus Christ: spiritual power and guidance. Source of the miraculous, upon which individuals recognize and develop their own spiritual treasure for guidance through life.

Table discussion is about who Christ is to each participant. Share stories of spiritual encounter.

Week Three

Holy Scripture: God's love story between the divine and creation.

Table discussion is about the Bible, its interpretation and meaning.

Week Four

The soul: people are spiritual in nature, the true self that has a body with mind included, awaiting use and development from a divine source of love and in need of nurture and guidance. Stories of faith are again shared to evidence the soul and its spiritual treasure.

Table discussion is about people's perception of the soul and life experience of divine love and power. This includes the sharing of faith stories.

Week Five

The Book of Common Prayer: a manual and gift from all Christian centuries, ordering time for spiritual discernment and growth, giving order for public and private worship

Table discussion is about people's experience of corporate worship and their feelings about liturgical worship, using the church calendar for both personal and church life.

Week Six

The Holy Eucharist: central to Christian worship, combining word and sacrament, individual and community. Connecting the senses of hearing, seeing, tasting, feeling, and doing—in communion with the divine and each other.

Table discussion is about participants' experience of the Holy Eucharist and how it affects their lives.

Week Seven

Church music: a beautiful part of creation that unites people and touches the soul in every life occasion. It transcends all cultures and has the power to lift spirits.

Table discussion is about how music reinforces the spiritual and how it influences and inspires each person. (You may wish to have hymnals on the tables.)

Week Eight

The cross: a necessity for secular as well as sacred life. The divine witness and scope of love.

Table discussion is about the crosses each person carries. What does it feel like to carry them? Do we have experiences of setting them down and walking away from them?

Week Nine

Holy Baptism and the Baptismal Covenant: the place of formal Christian initiation and the guidance for a pilgrimage through life. (Note the previously suggested alternative schedule by having the lecture first and then discussion.)

Table discussion is about the five guides to Christian living—community, penitence, sharing, serving, and promoting fairness.

Week Ten

Prayer: connecting thought, feeling, and action with the divine. Types of prayer and prayer practices offered.

Table discussion is about participants' experiences of prayer.

Week Eleven

The church: both its global presence and the particular denomination of the church hosting the class. The body of Christ on earth, commissioned to be blessed to bless in pursuit of God's kingdom on earth.

Table discussion is about denominations and the identity and purpose of all churches.

Week Twelve

Stewardship: talent, time, and treasure. Stewardship as the path to spiritual growth and service.

Table discussion is about time, talent, and treasure as they relate to our spiritual lives.

Week Thirteen

Church tour: how architecture shapes the spiritual through the eye. Significance of layout, glass, altar, pulpit, baptismal font, and cross.

Group discussion is about how architecture can shape one's faith.

Week Fourteen

Services of baptism, confirmation, reception and reaffirmation of baptismal vows: the content and expectation are explained, together with the role of the bishop. This is in preparation for those seeking church membership.

Table discussion is about individual questions, especially for those desiring church membership.

Week Fifteen

Review the special service of Christian initiation and reaffirmation.

Table discussion is devoted to individual questions and thoughts.

This week: Service of Christian initiation or reaffirmation with the bishop presiding. This could be a midweek occasion.

Follow-up Class

For new members or any others interested, an overview of ministry opportunities in congregational and personal life.

In lieu of table discussion, church members leading various areas of ministry are present to answer questions and extend invitations for participation.

Follow-up Class

Evangelism and how to engage those who may become new seekers of the spiritual. How worship and outreach ministries give a pathway for explorers of faith.

Table discussion is about how each person experiences evangelism, including how each person has come into association with the church.

As mentioned, this schedule is highly flexible, and it is tweaked at Heavenly Rest every time it is offered. The structure—how many sessions, how long they are, and their content—will take different shapes in different congregations.

FINAL THOUGHTS

The Rev. Luke Back, the rector of Heavenly Rest, assessed and evaluated this formation process after its first use in 2015. He wrote:

Connecting people to one another and God is the mission of Heavenly Rest and remains the fundamental role of any religion. Finding a key that awakens in the newcomer an awareness of the presence of Christ in the other is effective evangelism. After years of offering high-quality confirmation classes that shared many treasures of the church, something seemed incomplete and unfinished. An intentional focus on deepening personal relationships was elusive. Our New Member Formation Class model turned out to be a key we were missing, a gateway to a subtle sublime power of the Body of Christ.

The success of this new endeavor demanded leadership. Team-building meetings each week for two months converted us into a confident group of apostles. In the long run, Christianity is not only about discovering the guidance and grace of Episcopal tradition. Christianity at its truest and deepest is living life in the presence of God, just as the gospel reveals through the life, death, and resurrection of Jesus. Our classes helped unlock some of that healing power, its promise of forgiveness, the awareness of sacred beauty, the sanctification of the suffering, and the mystery of love.

Such is the story of one place. The keys are team development, peer engagement and a theological approach that affirms the spiritual birthright—a soul awaiting development—of every person. The entire process centers on how spiritual growth begins and continues. Clergy members focus on the fundamentals of the faith with those who are most eager to be engaged in basics. Clergy are drawn closer to their own call to Holy Orders, and feel they are more deeply transmitting Christ as the source of that call to their table mentors as well as newcomers. In essence this mirrors the vision of what they wanted to do once ordained. Lay persons grow exponentially in their faith. Clergy understand in powerful ways that all people are ministers of the gospel, not just the ordained. And clergy and lay leaders develop closer relationships and deeper mutual respect.

Not in isolation and individually, but in community and for the building of greater community, people find, revel in, and appreciate the spiritual treasure that God already has given them and that God wishes to give them in greater abundance. The classes do not use of fear or threat of judgment, but acceptance of each person as an act of love and mutual respect (the example of the divine). The classes do not deny the trials of life but lift up the cross as a way to sanctify any situation. And the classes show Christ to be center of our spirituality—the Christ who blesses and who challenges each of us to grow for the purpose of blessing others.

REFLECT AND RESPOND

- What do you think of the concept of Christianity being "caught"?

- What kind of divine encounters have you had?

- What was your Christian formation like? How comprehensive was it?

- How well equipped are you to verbalize what Christ has done and continues to do for you in non-theological or non-religious terms?

- Would you like to be a table mentor on a Christian formation team? Why or why not?

- How is Christian formation done in your congregation? How would you rate its effectiveness?

- How well does new church membership in your congregation prepare that person for a Christian pilgrimage through life?

- Do you desire a more productive way to grow spiritually?

CHAPTER 3
RECLAIMING **THE TEAM**

W hy does this model of Christian formation use leadership teams? Study after study shows that peer learning is highly effective, in classrooms, in businesses and in civic life. Peer learning makes people active participants, establishing them as co-leaders among their groups. In this setting, participants listen not only for information but also contemplate how they can respond to the needs implicit in the table conversation and the questions posed. They are active, not passive participants, and they become more deeply invested in their own call as a Christ-follower called to bless others.

But there's a second reason to work with a leadership team: Jesus used this methodology. His disciples constituted a leadership team; Jesus entrusted this team with the early nurture of the church and the perpetuation of his teachings. Day by day, the team of disciples was exposed to Jesus, his ways, his purpose, and his message. They discovered his vision—the kingdom of God at hand. They discovered his mission—to assist people in their need as a means of fulfilling that vision. They participated with him in his mission. Indeed, Jesus' teachings were so startling and his behavior so striking that the disciples needed to talk among themselves in order to reflect on, make sense of, and integrate into themselves all that they were seeing and hearing.

As a part of their training, Jesus sent them out two by two, subteams capable of far more than working solo. To do this ministry, they had to articulate together his vision, use his methodology, and rely upon the resources he conferred on them. After the resurrection, Peter and John worked together to proclaim Jesus at the Jerusalem temple. Paul, Barnabas, and John Mark went on a missionary journey. Later, Barnabas continued to partner with John Mark for his team to return to Cyprus, and Paul recruited Silas to work as one of his partners. At Derbe, Paul and Silas added Timothy to the team. Often others are named in the course of Paul's travels, leaving us to believe the team kept growing. For instance, in Corinth Paul, Silas, and Timothy added Priscilla and Aquila to the team as they made their way to Ephesus.

The first century was not the last time the church taught and spread the faith in teams. The Celts, for example, used this same approach. In his book *The Celtic Way of Evangelism*, author George G. Hunter III documents how monastic teams brought Christianity from Ireland to Iona in northern Scotland and eventually to the north of England in the seventh century. Their model followed a method Saint Patrick developed for the conversion of the Irish. Teams of monks penetrated the Irish culture where there were no cities or villages. The Celtic monks lived among the people. They worked, prayed, shared, taught, and helped those in their midst. Newcomers were made to feel at ease and told that they were important as God's children. They were given a place within the formation team community.

Hunter documents an ancient Chinese poem that captures the essence of this way of evangelism. It goes:

> Go to the people.
> Live among them.
> Learn from them.
> Love them.
> Start with what they know.
> Built on what they have.[ii]

This team method of evangelism recognizes that it is in first being loved that people become open to learning about the source of that love. This is the insight my model of spiritual transmission seeks to harness—we teach the faith in teams, not primarily to save the pastor work or to make ourselves feel good because we've aligned the church with the business world's so-called "best practices," but because it is through engagement with others that people become curious about Jesus.

EXPLORATION

Lance Taylor was recruited to be a table leader at the Church of the Heavenly Rest not long after becoming a church member. Prior to membership both he and his wife were spiritually awakened while tending to his wife's ailing grandmother. Her burial service at Heavenly Rest led Lance to discover a home in the Episcopal church. Having attended the new member formation classes under the last use of the old lecture-only model and serving as a team leader in the new model, Lance was able

---

[ii] George Hunter, *The Celtic Way of Evangelism: How Christianity Can Reach the West…Again* (Nashville: Abingdon Press, 2000), 120.

to compare the two approaches. "I really liked the new format," he says. "It let us talk about God with each other rather than only having us listen to a lecturer. It opened my heart when hearing others. Stories about faith and use of faith invigorate people. I could see others changing even as I myself was fed. I knew I was onto something very special." Commenting on the spiritual impact this had, he says, "I learned how to pray more effectively. I have come closer to Christ and to my wife and children. I have less fear and I have felt loved. I see new beauty in everything. Money has become less important, I've gotten rid of a lot of clutter, and I am more confident."

Most of you have already taken the first step in forming a Christian formation team without even realizing it—you have recognized the need for change. You are already at step two, which raises the question, "How?" This chapter is a tool to aid local exploration, planning, and implementation.

Forming a leadership team begins with one person. Next, engage a colleague. When possible, choose one with whom you already have a bond in terms of vision, mission, and core values. Say, "Let's try to strengthen the spiritual basics in our church" and then add, "I've found this book that gives a model of how we can do it." If lay, you approach your clergy or another lay person. If clergy, you approach a lay person or another clergy staff member. You two become peers, bonded together in mission, who then recruit some additional peers with the potential for the same outlook and vision. Together, you reflect upon some of the places in which God is calling for growth and deeper enagement. This initial exploration can bear fruit, even if you decide it's not the right time for your church to launch a basic Christianity course. Pondering these questions together with others is itself a way of loving the Lord in conversation and in fellowship.

If you and your partner or small team feel led to the next step of hosting a basic Christianity class, you will feel some fear. This is natural. Yet the rewards are so great—and the act of stepping out into what we don't know, and feeling fear while doing so, is an act with a long Christian pedigree. The results—the nourishment of rich spiritual soil in your congregation, church members, newcomers, and yourself—are incomparable, truly a pearl of great price.

LAUNCHING THE TEAM

If the idea for the course originates with lay people, they need to involve a clergy person fairly soon. Then, together, the small core of leaders become immersed in the vision. Remembering that growth occurs in stages and over time, the rush for numbers should not govern this process. If it takes ten months or a year for the right leadership team to emerge, so be it.

The first step is to create a small nucleus that will guide the initiative. Before expanding for recruitment of an entire team, many of the details should already be in place. Training times should be established so that potential team members can determine whether they can accommodate the schedule. It is also helpful to outline other expectations for team membership so they will know the full picture before committing.

Recruited team members participate in three training sessions. In addition to being present weekly as table mentors, team members also meet weekly apart from the class sessions for feedback, critique, and further theological and spiritual reflection. This is precious time, uniting and bonding a team whose members have internalized the projected vision, what is expected from the team, and how implementation will take place.

It has been my experience that when recruiting for a formation team, I have hardly ever been turned down. Laity are hungry, really hungry, for spiritual and theological conversation with their clergy leaders. Consequently, recruiting and working with a team is a fantastic experience. Those most active will relish this kind of opportunity and challenge, and make time to fulfill the commitment. Still, I recommend recruiting additional people because you will need table substitutes—perfect attendance among team members is not a workable reality any more than for newcomers.

Recruiting is often the easiest part of this entire process. People will respond. Take the story of Kathy Balch, a lifelong Episcopalian who was delighted to join the formation team at Heavenly Rest. Even though she was quite active, this invitation offered an expansive kind of growth. "I was honored when asked," she says. "It offered new opportunity in an area basic to my faith. It was a thrill to be offered this opportunity. As a result, through my training and participation with fellow team members as well as newcomers, my faith has been deepened and broadened. Talking with others lifted me out of my more privatized spirituality and opened to me a much broader world." Kathy's story has been echoed by others who have become team members.

Once recruitment is complete, the team begins its work in earnest. The first team meeting is an ideal time to review theology, upon which everything else depends. The priest should lead this session. When doing this personally, I begin with Christ who came as Jesus to transform lives and lift life heavenward, present, future, and forever. Christ is spiritual power and guidance; the kingdom of God at hand was his stated vision. I move from Christ to the church, the body that Christ summoned into being. Referring to the church as a community of miraculous expectation helps it be recognized by its spiritual rather than institutional identity. That the Christian calling is to those beyond its doors—the ecclesially unattached, so to speak—moves the faithful from self-centered church maintenance into mission, be that outreach to the spiritually hungry in evangelism, or outreach to those with various kinds of material needs, or outreach that seeks to create a more just society.

This meeting gives a forum for a rector or senior pastor to articulate his or her own theological approach to the Christian faith. Often this is helpful to clergy because it gives incentive for them to evaluate themselves, something they need but sometimes fail to do. It also allows those most active in a congregation to coalesce around a common vision and mission.

I also use this first meeting as a time to briefly discuss biblical interpretation, to give the team members (and later to prospective newcomers) a powerful, sensitive, comprehensive, and inspirational way to interpret the Bible. If the gap between the reality of what people face in daily life and a theology based on "what the Bible says" literally is not addressed satisfactorily, new or renewed Christians will be ill-prepared to reap the divine promises that come from scripture. Clergy leaders have a sensitive and tricky role here, as clergy often do in Christian education (especially Christian education that involves lay participation): they have to firmly present what they take to be sound theology, but also leave space for lay leaders to have their own views. As discussed in more detail in the next chapter, the tone is one of mutual respect. My observation is that rigid theological separation over scripture, though it may be well intended, is a major factor in the decline of Christianity.

At the next session, each member of the team shares part of his or her faith story. Often this will be a new experience for team members. This session provides a safe setting for identifying, verbalizing, and building upon the spiritual treasure that each has accumulated. I have used the story of delivering flowers on Easter when I was a teenager as an example of faith sharing. I have also sometimes told my wife's story of growth in spiritual treasure (with her permission, of course!). Specifically, I recount the spiritual growth Barbara experienced as I was leaving a job in industry to attend seminary and prepare for ordination. Barbara was willing to teach school during my three years in seminary.

My seminary was in Berkeley, California. Barbara's first interview was in Oakland where she arrived dressed in hat and gloves. She was told that there weren't any jobs currently available but one might possibly open up. The next day she went to a nearby community and heard the same reply: No jobs. When she left that office, Barbara heard a distinct voice saying, "Call Oakland." To her astonishment, she spotted a telephone booth. She called Oakland and found that they were trying to find her, but couldn't because she had left no local contact number. A job had just opened, but they required an interview. Promising to get there as quickly as possible, she looked around and, once again with delightful astonishment, spotted a taxi parked immediately in front at the curb nearby. Mind you, this was not a big hotel or major airport, a place where cabs are usually parked, but rather the equivalent of a cab idling in front of an antique shop or hair parlor.

The superintendent in Oakland wasn't too comfortable with her accent—part Arkansas South, part Texas drawl; he wondered how well her pupils would understand her—but he was willing to overlook what he considered a minor flaw and continued to pursue the job exploration. The next step was an interview with the local principal. At the conclusion of that interview, the principal asked Barbara what brought her to the Bay Area. It turned out the principal was an Episcopalian. Most likely she would have gotten the job anyway, but this was a bit of icing on the cake.

Most certainly this experience could be explained as a series of coincidences and a bit of luck. But my wife and I see the miraculous in it. We see that which inspires and feeds the soul. We see that which contributes to the building of an inner strength that supports, sustains, encourages, and anticipates even more. It is something that is never taken away. When difficult times occur as they always do, this story helps us persevere. The experience has been a part of my wife's spiritual treasure, and mine too, ever since.

This kind of personal story sets the stage for others to share a story of faith. I like to tell my wife's story because it illustrates so clearly that what we're after here is a lens—the lens that allows a person to see ordinary coincidence as, in fact, miraculous and spiritual. People's stories will vary greatly. Some people may seem to have nothing to share because they have never given this much thought or have never been challenged to identify divine action in their lives. This arena provides a safe forum to explore such experiences. In sharing, the spirits of all are raised and new insights gained. Members of the leadership team leave this meeting cognitively connected to their inner spiritual treasure, more deeply connected with one another, and prepared to lead similar conversations at their tables.

The final training session focuses on the nuts and bolts of procedure—when and where the classes will be held, when to arrive, how the room will be set up, what materials will be needed, what questions will be used, how valuable it is to wear name tags. It's important to remind people that the entire course is a supreme act of love, much like having guests come to one's home. Those with Cursillo or other renewal movement experiences will recognize the notion that paying attention to detail is in fact an expression of love. People who come to something new often feel anxious, the first act of ministry is to dispel these anxieties with happy smiles and warm welcomes. Beyond that, a well-prepared and well-executed class is another act of love. Those coming deserve the best, as nothing less than the enrichment of their lives now and forever is the goal. It is a glorious task and deserves our best.

The church members who are lecturing but who are not part of the table mentors group can also be included in the training sessions; this will give them a vision of the entire process—its purpose and its methodology. Or they can be gathered separately and given an overview of the process. It may be helpful to ask the lecturers to build into their lectures vignettes about how what they teach translates into their daily lives. Also, remind lecturers to comment on how the material they're teaching influences how they worship. For instance, the lecturer on prayer can share personal prayer practices. The lecturer on the cross can talk about how she thinks about Holy Eucharist or how he experiences Good Friday. When giving a church tour, the leader can talk about how the stained glass windows or the gleaming wood of the pews has shaped her worship.

The next step is identifying and inviting newcomers and others who may want to explore the Christian faith. I encourage both personal invitations as well as churchwide announcements. You never know who might be in need of this type of formation. Include with the invitation details about what to expect, class schedules, and an outline of topics. Make sure you have a system in place to follow up with those who have expressed an interest. This act of love shows that you look upon anyone expressing interest in learning more about Christianity as important and worthy of the best.

A weekly team meeting once classes begin is essential for continuity. Identify and share signs of the Holy Spirit's influence. Critique the previous class. Prepare for the next class session. It's appropriate, too, to include brief discussions of newcomers with an eye toward noticing whether any has a special need, and if so, what, and whether anything can be done to address that need. Review attendance. Possible calls to absentees can be assigned. Make adjustments as needed. Ideas for future classes can be noted as learnings continue to unfold. Include a time for biblical and/or theological reflection as a means of continuing spiritual nurture for team members. Along the way, lay leaders will notice they are becoming closer to one another and to the clergy who are on the team. These meetings amount to spiritual embellishment and pastoral care for the whole team. Everyone involved looks forward to the weekly check-in.

Like all start-ups, this takes time and effort, and the process will have its ups and downs. Many clergy act as individual proprietors and not team captains; for them, the learning curve will be enormous. The beauty for clergy is that they don't have to scale that curve alone—there will be a team with more than enough insight, help, and skill to live into the needed shifts.

And the rewards are huge. Secular models confirm this. Physicians form teams with other physicians, each of which also have physician's assistants and nurses. Dentists likewise. Detective work is done mostly by teams. Newscasters work in teams under a lead announcer. Churches use teams for capital fund drives, empowering lay persons for leading roles. The formation team simply shifts the task from fundraising to gospel transmission and the miraculous transformation of lives!

The formation goal is that each newcomer will be led into a fuller, healthier, holier life in Christ through development of spiritual treasure. This is the overriding vision. Hopefully those who come will become new or renewed disciples who will be emboldened by receiving "the promise of the Father" (Luke 24:49). The formation team's task is to provide a welcoming environment, engaging presentations, and personal witnesses for newcomers to have encounters with Christ. Hopefully, newcomers will feel drawn toward a serving ministry in the congregation. Hopefully, they'll leave the course better equipped to become more responsible at home and in the community. And hopefully, they will be so engaged and enthusiastic that they will eagerly reach out to their spiritually unattached friends and invite them to a church ministry or activity as an act of evangelism.

Lance Taylor, the relative newcomer who quickly joined the leadership team at Church of the Heavenly Rest, has influenced others to explore the Christian faith. Working in retail where he meets the public daily, his personality is such that people quickly trust him and often seek his advice. Sometimes they ask about his faith and church. This opens a door for him to invite them to explore. He has found, as I have, that people are spiritually hungry. And the most holy approach in evangelism is through reaching out to people in their need through conversation they initiate. This approach allows Lance and others to talk about their faith in a way that comes across as personal interest as opposed to promotion of the church. While it's wonderful to invite people to church, how much better is the invitation if you know there is a formation team well prepared to welcome, love, listen, receive, accept, and encourage them—whether they choose to become church members or not! Nothing in the congregation's life is more important than Christian formation for both adults and youth. This team model, utilizing peer engagement, is a way to make it happen in a joyful and powerful way.

Beyond local Christian formation efforts, peer engagement and team formation can be huge tools for dioceses or other regional church judicatories. Clergy assemblies do not have to follow the usual talking-head model. Having clergy make peer presentations on what they are accomplishing gives bishops or other judicatory leaders the opportunity to highlight places that have become models of health and hope. As presenters prepare, they have the opportunity to evaluate what is working well and why. Participants can engage in discussion as a means of seeking improvement. Likewise bishops or other judicatory leaders can introduce the formation team model for evangelism, encouraging or, if possible, directing clergy to implement such an initiative. Sharing of faith stories should also be a part of the overall agenda.

THE JOYS THAT AWAIT

Joy, really deep joy, comes through this team process. At the congregational level the first joy is having parishioners respond so happily when asked to join the formation team, impressed and thrilled to be recruited for such a significant undertaking. Most lay ministry jobs do not require engagement with faith essentials. This does—and that requirement is appealing to lay people. So the entire process gets off to a buoyant beginning through the simple but profound invitation to be part of the formation team.

The second joy is the teaching of the team recruits. Most clergy like to teach, and in this setting the vision, mission, and core values of the congregation can be articulated and reiterated. If such a vision, mission, and core value statement does not exist, it should. A sample vision could be the title of this book— *Reclaiming Christianity*. Added on could be something like "in an increasingly secular society." The lay team will be thrilled to be lay pastors (or whatever name they are given). My experience is that they will eagerly anticipate their training and assignments each week. They will look forward to the theological reflection and sharing their own stories of faith. They will relish the nuts and bolts of how each session runs and appreciate their own growth as the team meets weekly after classes begin. There is joy for all, and each will contribute to the joy of all the others.

Another enormous joy, especially for clergy, is the sense that they are not alone in ministry but are working in tandem with the formation team. No longer is this singularly important congregational function dependent on the solo leadership of the priest but rather a deep pool of active, engaged leaders. There is no way to quantify the joy and growth that may come from having a lay group involved directly with their own spiritual journeys, the depth of the Christian tradition, and the spiritual growth of people receiving Christian formation. In the Episcopal Church, the ministry of the laity is often ballyhooed but rarely does that engagement take the laity into the heavy-lifting of Christian formation.

Engaging laity in formation team ministry utilizes laypeople's developed skills, teaches them new ones, and—as a secondary but very real benefit—releases clergy time to work on other tasks, such as pastoral care and homiletical preparation.

Furthermore, it's simply not healthy for clergy to spearhead Christian formation by themselves—it's healthy neither for the clergy, nor for the newcomers desiring a better life. This is not to criticize clergy competence, but to point out that Christian formation is a beginning from which new members continue to grow as long as they live. If that formation is really powerful, equipping them to pray, worship, engage scripture, deal with the manifold issues of life, create deep relationships with fellow Christians, and find a place in ministry, aren't those newcomers then grown into lay leaders who can help form other laypeople? Spiritual treasure abounds. Joy.

So far the joy has come to the formation team of clergy and lay leaders from their own interaction, preparation, and planning. Great joy comes from engaging newcomers. They come to church and to this class as explorers, anticipating something good (though they may also feel fearful or anxious or unsure of themselves and their surroundings). A team can far better deliver basic Christianity than can a pastor teaching alone, for a newcomer's needs are on many levels. When they find their longings and needs addressed, their joy skyrockets and their gratitude soars. Even with a lecture-only method of membership preparation, new members are often among the happiest in a congregation—because they're in that rare and blissful space of new discovery. With lectures plus table discussion rich in exchange, their joy will be far greater. And, as is so often true in the Christian life, that joy expands itself—newcomers' joy creates joy for formation team members.

Still another joy from this team approach comes from knowing that diverse and varied expressions of Christianity are being presented to newcomers. While Christ is always the means of conversion, community is the context for conversion. The formation team becomes the church in miniature into which the newcomer enters. It is the highest aspiration of calling because what is presented on behalf of and in witness to divine power, presence, and love is so penetrating. What more significance is there in life than supporting others in their spiritual growth and knowing you have been faithful with the talents the Lord left with you for investment?

Elyse and Patrick Lewis began worshiping at Heavenly Rest about a year before attending the Christian formation classes. "We didn't know what to expect," says Elyse. "Within two weeks of classes, we felt very comfortable, welcomed, and connected at Heavenly Rest. By the third week we were excited, looking forward to the class. We were touched by the sincerity of everyone there. Although we already had faith, we both felt closer to God. At home, we now pray together as well as separately.

"We also invite others to church and feel very comfortable in doing so. We share our experience with friends. Two couples have come already, just five months after we joined. Another important thing has happened too. We've been married five years and although we have always wanted to expand our family, it has been 'some time in the future.' We now feel more confident to move to that next stage of our lives." Such is the joy and power two newcomers have found through the team formation process. They have greater faith, deeper spirituality, and more confidence—plus, they have more friends of all ages.

Judy Daniels, another of those going through the formation experience at the Church of the Heavenly Rest, says she "became thirsty to learn more and wanted to be more involved in ministry." She says the classes helped her to take her prayer life more seriously and made her feel she was in a good place to nurture body, mind, and soul. People like Judy have become more equipped to live in loving response to the God who calls them to bring God's blessing to others.

A final joy is having so many fed. The spiritual life of clergy, lay team members, and newcomers alike are nurtured through the formation team and its ministry. Sharing stories of faith builds faith. Deepening faith relationships among the team and beginning faith relationships with newcomers builds the church. All participants become more fully equipped, fulfilled, engaged, and confident. This not only leavens the people taking or leading the class, but the congregation as well. Over time, the congregation finds its life and witness deepened, more textured, and more vibrant.

FINAL THOUGHTS

Team recruitment, training, and commissioning is effective because it provides an organized way for congregations to be intentional about what so often gets left undone or poorly done for lack of a more coherent method of gospel transmission. What is offered here affirms that the gospel is about hope—hope for divine power, hope for healthy, spiritually equipped people, hope for productive transformations in life, hope for love that affirms and builds confidence, and hope for personal growth and the ability to transmit the source of that gift to others. There is nothing more positive for hope than hopeful people, people who are optimistic and confident about what they are doing. In the church this means that the fruits of the Spirit mentioned in Galatians 5:22-23—love, joy, peace, patience, kindness, generosity, faithfulness, gentleness, and self-control—abound. So what is offered here builds on the gospel vision of hope and creates a way to transmit it through a team. The effect is to create a huge pool of energy that spreads out in all directions and dimensions.

REFLECT AND RESPOND

- What kind of team experience have you enjoyed outside of church? Why? In the church? Why?

- What do you think of a Christian formation team as outlined here? Is it attractive to you? Why or why not?

- How well are lay persons utilized for in-depth, spiritually based ministry in your congregation?

- Would knowing your congregation has a strong Christian team help you with evangelism? How?

- Could other team-type ministries in your congregation be strengthened by having a spiritual nurture component where stories of faith are shared?

- To what extent are team ministries already functioning in your congregation? Do any use spiritually based peer engagement as a means of soul nurture?

CHAPTER 4
RECLAIMING **SCRIPTURE**

ntroducing newcomers to scripture is a key part of initiating them into the Christian spiritual life. Many people dip their toes into church with either no knowledge of scripture, ambivalence about scripture, or downright negative feelings about scripture. These feelings include fear or the belief that the Bible is simply a book of "thou shalt nots" that often gets hijacked by one political agenda or another. Or, if they do know the Bible, they don't know how to respond to those passages that seem to contradict what they know to be true. My hope is that we teach people to view Holy Scripture as a love story between God and the created order. To be sure, a love story between God and the created order is not all there is to say about scripture—and certainly, Christians will always disagree about various points of biblical interpretation. But let's ground those disagreements in a love we all know to be abundant, unmerited, and testified to by the Bible. Let's ground those disagreements in the soil of inspired testimony to God's love for all that God made.

I want us to craft a narrative about scripture that encourages all Christians to proclaim that scripture is authoritative— not just the pride of evangelicals. Too often, Christians concerned for social justice do not publicly reference scripture as their motivation for this work. But civil rights and recognizing the worth of all people are grounded in scripture. My hope is that the idea of scripture as a love story between God and creation will draw people of all theological stripes to the table, where we can read, tussle over, and pray with the scriptures together. Reading together will always yield more than reading in self-selected affinity groups. We will learn from one another as we read the Bible through the lens of love.

Recall the story I offered earlier about the young mother taking her two children to church. Then think about how that mother can become equipped, through her church—through God's people and disciples of Christ—to read scripture as an aid to her self-understanding. Think about that mother reading with so much insight and curiosity that she wants her children to read the Bible, too. How will she handle passages like the one when Abraham passes Sarah, his wife, off to Pharaoh as his sister? What about those passages that focus on God's wrath and the threat of hell? What about the passages that uphold slavery or tell wives to be subject to their husbands?

Like all of life, scripture is complex and at times ambiguous, as when God condemns only to reverse and affirm. The complexity is not (nor should it be) erased when we view scripture as a love story—but the complexity is usefully framed by the precept of a love story. God does undoubtedly get angry with God's people. But there are many moments that warm the divine heart. Warmth is stronger than the cold. Light supersedes the dark. Good triumphs over the bad. Hope trumps despair. Beauty evolves from chaos. This is the scope and power of the divine through God's Word when interpreted by love.

JESUS AS INTERPRETER

For a guide to interpreting scripture as a love story, we look to Jesus. This springs from Jesus' own summation of scripture as the summary of the law. "You shall love the Lord your God with all your heart, and with all your soul, and with all your mind," he says. "This is the greatest and first commandment. And a second is like it: 'You shall love your neighbor as yourself.' On these two commandments hang all the law and the prophets" (Matthew 22:37-39). Jesus' summation of scripture provides a guide for us as week to read, learn, and inwardly digest.

Jesus personifies love. And Jesus' words and actions overflow with love. To wit, his vision of the kingdom of God at hand, now, in the present: "I came that they may have life, and have it abundantly," Jesus says (John 10:10). His cross is a revelation of the extent of divine love and a model by which the faithful should live in the pursuit of a significant life. His resurrection is a testimony of divine supremacy and love. He challenges complacency and is champion of all forms of neglect, injustice, and degradation. In a word, he came and comes as spiritual power and guidance for every age and circumstance. He epitomizes health and wholeness. He is the way, truth, and life, available to all as a personification of love.

Perhaps nowhere in scripture is the essence of God as one who loves unconditionally more evident than in the parable of the prodigal son (Luke 15:11-32). The son asks for his inheritance and receives it. He goes away and squanders the entire inheritance. He finally "comes to himself" and returns home penitent, expecting nothing beyond a frugal means of survival. Yet the father, even when the son is still far away on the road, recognizes him and runs to meet him. He is thrilled to see the son whom he never expected to see again. "Quickly, bring out a robe—the best one—and put it on him; put a ring on his finger and sandals on his feet. And get the fatted calf and kill it, and let us eat and celebrate, for this son of mine was dead and is alive again; he was lost and is found!" All is forgiven, even though the family wealth has been diminished and the son returns destitute and in disgrace.

God forgives, even though there is an unfairness in doing so. The elder brother is acutely aware of this unfairness and makes his displeasure known. He is the dutiful one, expecting the reward of one who has been loyal, dutiful, respectful, responsible, and upright. He readily recognizes this unfairness when the one who has strayed seems to receive a far greater reward. But Jesus pursues the way of love, even when that love is at odds with human calculation.

When confronted by the Canaanite woman whose child is sick, Jesus, at first interpreting scripture more narrowly and more literally, tries to turn her away (Matthew 15: 21-28). He tells her that he has come only to the lost sheep of the house of Israel. But through the application of love as a basis for understanding scripture—and challenged yet again by a mother's concern for her child—Jesus reverses his response and heals the child. Confronted by obvious human need, Jesus chooses a different, more loving way. A similar occasion occurs when Jesus meets a Samaritan woman at a well. He chooses to speak to a woman who is a religious outcast. He engages her in conversation with love, and in turn, she responds to him. She returns to town and proclaims his name. The transformation initiated by Jesus turns her into an early gospel evangelist, all because he let himself be led by love and the spirit of scripture rather than the letter (John 4:4-42). He continually heals on the sabbath; he looks at the Ten Commandments through the lens of love, reconfiguring the Decalogue's sabbath command. He tells those who challenge him: "The sabbath was made for humankind, and not humankind for the sabbath" (Mark 2:27). Furthermore, Jesus explains to his adversaries that he has come to fulfill and not abolish the law (Matthew 5:17). He honors the past but in a way that uses love as a basis for change. Interpreting scripture through love does not give Jesus nor us a license to reinterpret beyond the bounds of reason those passages whose literal meanings we do not like. What it does is to let its sacred pages be interpreted by its overarching message—being God's love for all of creation.

Writing to the Corinthians, Saint Paul identifies love as "a still more excellent way" (1 Corinthians 12:31):

> Love is patient; love is kind; love is not envious or boastful or arrogant or rude. It does not insist on its own way; it is not irritable or resentful; it does not rejoice in wrongdoing, but rejoices in the truth. It bears all things, believes all things, hopes all things, endures all things. Love never ends (1 Corinthians 13:4-8).

Love as mutual respect is at the heart of this passage. Love as the interpretive tool enables readers to deal with passages of scripture that seem to contradict love. I'm thinking of passages such as, "Whoever comes to me and does not hate father and mother, wife and children, brothers and sisters, yes, and even life itself, cannot be my disciple" (Luke 14:26). One way to approach this passage is to recognize that Jesus says he is to be first priority, superseding family relationships and even one's personal life. Another view recognizes that Jesus believes the end of all was at hand, and only those with him would survive the chaos. Hence people, for survival, would have to put that survival over family or personal life. Love does not necessarily offer a single, definitive interpretation of a given biblical passage.

But the lens of love can help us read even those passages that seem, at first blush, unloving.

It is apropos to remember that the Bible uses "The Word" in two different and distinct contexts. One is scripture itself, the Bible, known as the Word of God. The other equates "The Word" with Christ "In the beginning was the Word," is the way Saint John's Gospel starts (John 1:1). Christ is "The Word" who appears as a human in the incarnation. Consequently, it is highly appropriate to interpret "The Word of God" of scripture with "The Word of God" that is Christ. This means the written word of scripture must adhere to the Word made flesh, Christ; Scripture, in other words, must conform to the God who is love. As Saint Augustine wrote in *On Christian Teaching*, "Anyone who thinks that he has understood the scriptures, or any part of them, but cannot by his understanding build up this double love of God and neighbor, has not yet succeeded in understanding them."

OVERCOMING PITFALLS

From Reformation times until now, scripture has been used to foster division among the faithful. In no way does this diminish the inspirational power people gain through the reading of the Bible. In no way does this impinge upon scripture's potency to transform lives. It simply means that division among Christians and between Christian bodies has become the norm over the past five hundred years. Consequently, at a time when Christianity's influence is diminishing and when churches are shrinking, it is imperative for the faithful of all traditions to seek ways of working together in mutual respect based on love.

Reading the Bible through love offers the prospect of uniting the various strands of Christianity—even when we sometimes deeply disagree. This approach allows scripture to guide churches and Christians to honor their differences in a positive and loving way. It holds a powerful, mutually supportive integrity that becomes a beautiful witness to those whom all Christians are called to serve. Reading through love does not rob Christians or various Christian traditions of a prerogative to interpret scripture in their own way—as long as mutual respect prevents them from excommunicating others.

Love anticipates disagreement—as the story of Adam and Eve makes clear. History, biblical and otherwise, is a record of conflict among peoples, nations, tribes, and ideas. Yet strangely and beautifully, love is the means by which people can disagree and continue to live in harmony. Living in tension with one another through love allows growth. All Christians, regardless of our other disagreements, pray the scriptural prayer known as the Lord's Prayer: "thy kingdom come, thy will be done, on earth as it is in heaven." Love triumphs.

Disagreement over issues like sexual orientation and the ordination of women is only a surface problem, albeit a major one. Interpretation of scripture is at the root. This is not so much the case in the Episcopal Church in the United States, since its move to permit ordination of women and marriage of same-sex couples. But it remains a huge problem within the Anglican Communion and in numerous other Christian bodies. In this context, it's crucial to remember that while churches have often fractured over biblical interpretation, the Bible has been used throughout history, and can be used now, as a guide for much-needed unity, without compromising denominational integrity or demanding unified agreement.

The Archbishop of Canterbury, titular head the Anglican Communion (which includes the Episcopal Church), has taken the initiative to deal with its threatened divisions by an appeal to love and respect. The archbishop presides at meetings of the communion's leaders (called primates) who represent the thirty-eight different and independent Anglican Churches worldwide. From their meeting in January of 2015 came this statement: "Over the past week the unanimous decision of the Primates was to walk together, however painful this is, and despite our differences, as a deep expression of our unity in the body of Christ." This decision to walk together was a response to an issue that cannot be resolved quickly. It provides a pathway on a global scale for Anglican Christians to answer the call to mission without separating from each other.

Although biblical interpretation was not mentioned as part of the 2015 statement, nonetheless biblical interpretation remains the root of disagreement. Those in favor of change fail to reference scripture as their authority, effectively surrendering "what the Bible says" to those who support inherited tradition. The rhetoric of civil rights (equality of all) is quoted by those who advocate change. But the authority of equality and all being made in the divine image comes straight from scripture. Not to say this seems like a sinful omission. This needs both recognition and correction. It identifies on a global scale that biblical interpretation is the root cause of issues of conflict.

By using love as a biblical mandate that can be claimed by all, conflicts on issues such as sexuality shift to a healthy discussion of what scripture expects. This discussion won't yield instant agreement, but it allows people who disagree about sexuality to see that they agree on something more important—God's love for all God made. All involved in this arena carry a heavy burden, but this too is a Christian calling. Each comes with strong faith. Each holds the Bible as authority. Thus it seems an appropriate step to move the center of discussion to scripture, interpreted by the Great Commandment.

Pope Francis seems to sense that the demonic dimension of denominational division is rooted in biblical interpretation. He does not use biblical reference as such to support what he does. He simply acts, and so often that action is modeled after what Jesus would do. In other words, his actions are a mode of biblical interpretation. He is living out the gospel, in a stance of love.

Just look at Pope Francis's demeanor. He is open, engaging, humble, loving, attending to the misused and weak. He is sensitive and passionate about this servant ministry. He is exposing a fresh and yet highly biblical expression of Christianity that is admirable, contagious, and uplifting. He is essentially ignoring vestiges of past prestige, exclusivity, pomposity, and adherence to church laws, all derived from a more narrow interpretation of holy writ, that not only restrict human behavior but have been used to condemn those who live outside its boundaries. His is a faith that revolves around the heart that then informs the mind.

SCRIPTURE AND ADAPTATION

Scripture itself is full of discussion of, and wisdom about, disagreement. Consider the fifth chapter of the Acts of the Apostles. In this narrative, Peter and John are brought before the high priest and his council because they refuse to stop proclaiming Jesus, something the council has ordered them to do. The apostles defy the order and the authorities want to kill them. But a well-respected teacher and Pharisee named Gamaliel asks for a private audience with his colleagues. He says:

Fellow Israelites, consider carefully what you propose to do to these men. For some time ago Theudas rose up, claiming to be somebody, and a number of men, about four hundred, joined him; but he was killed, and all who followed him were dispersed and disappeared. After him Judas the Galilean rose up at the time of the census and got people to follow him; he also perished, and all who followed him were scattered. So in the present case, I tell you, keep away from these men and let them alone; because if this plan or this undertaking is of human origin, it will fail; but if it is of God, you will not be able to overthrow them—in that case you may even be found fighting against God! (Acts 5:35-39)

In a word, Gamaliel counsels that matters of division be left to the Holy Spirit and given time to run a natural course. Those under the Spirit's guidance will ultimately prevail. This gives the struggle inside the community of faith a theological framework. The process delays making a universal decision, allows the competing claims to be held in tension, and leaves for a future time the resolution as experience is gained to give clarity. In the interim, love prevails.

Every generation deals with cultural change, and adjusting to that change is often difficult. It's understandable that people sometimes resist change—they don't do so for bad reasons, but rather they do so because they seek, for themselves and their communities, stability and calm. At the same time, every community has people who are welcoming change, who seek change, who are agents of change. Love provides a way to hold communities together in the midst of disagreements about change.

Scriptural interpretation was at the root of the huge conflict created in the early church over inclusion of Gentiles in the faith community. Acts 15:1-21 reveals the resolution that Gentiles could become Christians. While accepted as natural now, it wasn't then. The Gentiles were the hated enemies of Jews. The Greeks under Alexander the Great had conquered the Holy Land several centuries before Christ. With the Greeks later defeated and driven out in the years before the coming of Jesus, the Jews once again lost their independence and came under Gentile domination by the Romans. Since they hated their Roman oppressors, it is almost unimaginable to think that the early Jewish Christians would be open to Gentile inclusion. But that's exactly what happens. This unexpected reversal prompts Saint Peter to say in Acts 10:34-35, "I truly understand that God shows no partiality." Christianity made an enormous adaptation, initiated by a divine source, with authentication documented in scripture and writing interpreted by love.

When the second coming of Christ did not happen during the early church period, the essence of Christianity was challenged. The New Testament is laced with references to the imminent return of Christ. Jesus himself seems to imply he will return soon. Evidence that the earliest Christians sold their possessions and lived communally documents how Christians ordered their common life around this expectation (Acts 2:44-45). But the delay in Christ's coming continued year after year. As time unfolded Christians discarded their end-of-the-world communal structure. So, the very earliest of times reveal how Christians creatively adapted to changing circumstances. This required a re-examination of things Jesus said and did.

Even the creation of the New Testament itself illustrates dynamics of change in the early church. Early Christians hardly needed a Christian scripture if the end were imminent. When Christ didn't appear, his followers begin assembling recollections of Jesus and writings of early Christian leaders as their post-Jesus scripture. Until then their only scripture was the Old Testament. Various recollections of what Jesus said and did, together with letters and writings among early Christians, in time became the New Testament. This was adaptation to changing circumstances. Creating a new scripture was most certainly a necessary Christian imperative. Love motivated these changes, as the faithful made adjustments to address new circumstances and understandings.

I could fill this book with examples of Christians adapting to change—it's deep in our church DNA to face change and to deal with it—not without conflict, but always striving for love. Without equating new discovery as always for the good, adaptation creates a healthy pathway for the use of Gamaliel's guideline to wait upon the Holy Spirit for evaluation. This is not license to change at will but with biblical insight. Furthermore it should be a lesson from our own history that culture is not the enemy of faith but the front line of ever evolving discovery. Determining how to adapt to cultural discovery in a hallowed way, even though it presents daunting challenges, is a necessary Christian activity.

More modern times have myriad examples of how new discovery has radically changed culture. Consider emancipation from hard labor, made possible by inventions that allowed machines to reduce what previously had been done by humans. Improved means of transportation have given humanity geographical emancipation by enabling quick access to the entire world and even parts of outer space. Communication is such that humans can now connect instantly to anyone, anywhere. Medical advances have emancipated humanity from debilitating diseases and have made treatment of others much more advanced. While these efforts at emancipation have not directly affected biblical interpretation, they have nonetheless laid the foundation for gigantic cultural shifts that affect how Christians behave and what rules they follow.

The emancipation of slaves is another example of how scripture, interpreted through love, and supported by the biblical affirmation that all humans are not only equal but also made in the divine image, has enabled adaptation from older, harsher ways. So, too, the emancipation of women from the inherited cultural norms that expected them to keep house, raise children and be subservient to husbands has certainly challenged Christianity.

Then came the discovery of effective birth control. No discovery in human history has affected the social fabric of society more than this. For the first time ever, humans could enjoy the pleasures of sexual expression emancipated from the possibility of conception. Coupled with the discovery that sexual orientation is God-ordained and not rooted in human choice, this has set in motion a revolution that challenges the inherited concepts of family, marriage, and the practice of fornication.

In the twenty-first century, Christians in different parts of the world have different approaches to gender and sexuality. Many parts of the developing world have infrastructure that depends upon women to raise children and maintain a household. Since families are defined by the roles each sex contributes for survival, they cannot easily accommodate professional gender equality. Without gender parity, same-sex coupling is highly challenging. Knowing this, the loving approach of mutual respect seems all the more urgent for Christians. Rather than demonizing positions on these issues, the path forward is to hold the outcome in tension while persisting in love and in mutual respect of those with whom we fiercely disagree. Today's upheavals over gender and sexual issues are new in specifics but decidedly not new insofar as they partake of the age-old biblical pattern of living with disagreement and adapting to change in every generation.

Seen in light of this historic record, the present offers an opportunity for religious communities to use their differences as ways to explore emancipation, through love. This opens the way for newcomers to the church to see Christianity as creative, attractive, and restorative rather than static, out of touch, and restrictive. Love promotes toleration and respect between Christians and those who are not Christian. Love, in other words, is missionary in spirit and deed. And it is biblical to the core.

When I think of the Bible—when I think of how I want churchgoers to feel about, live with, and revere, the Bible—I picture the late Billy Graham and how he held the book high as God's Word, letting the pages sway as he preached. I'd like to see today's preachers do the same, holding the Bible high and letting the pages flutter as they proudly proclaim, "This book shows the way: the way of love, the way of examining reality in the light of new discovery, the way of claiming the future, the way of promoting the kingdom of God right now. This book has the answers to making faith relevant through the building of spiritual treasure, recognition of the soul, and fighting greed, corruption, and self-aggrandizement. Recognizing that society favors those with the most power and the growing focus on a 'me first' mentality, this book challenges us to serve and embrace the beauty of humility."

In *A New Kind of Christianity,* author Brian McLaren says that the Bible is a library of cultures and communities that trace their history back to Abraham, Isaac, and Jacob. There is variation, of course, in how those communities live with and testify to God. But unifying that library is the proclamation of God's call in love for people to be blessed to bless others. In this way the

Bible is constitutional as God's word interpreted by love, but not a constitution where truth comes from selected concepts and passages.

To reclaim a Christianity that reflects the values and methods of Jesus, we must look to scripture and interpret it by the call of being blessed to bless. The imperatives of blessing and love direct the good intentions, tremendous faith, goodwill, and personal spiritual treasure of the faithful into a higher vision. What is offered here is a broader way to see the Bible as a whole—and yet able to be condensed into the few words of the Great Commandment. In addition to using scripture for inspiration and challenge, I pray that it can become a beacon of unity, a way to transcend the temptation of separation and division.

FINAL THOUGHTS

Think about that young mother again who, because of her immersion in a local church, learns how to read scripture through the lens of love. When she reads to her children about Abraham and Sarah, and their journey to Egypt to survive a famine, the mother explains that times were different in those days. Abraham lied to Pharaoh to save their lives. Their survival depended upon their not being killed, which led Abraham to lie to Pharaoh. He didn't want to lie, but like so often happens today, he did it in order to survive. Because he (and Sarah too) survived, they continued to be God's chosen and kept alive the tiny community of faith that has grown into a worldwide community.

Or perhaps the mother is reading the parable of the rich man and Lazarus, where Lazarus goes to heaven upon death while the rich man goes to hell (Luke 16:19-31). The central focus of the parable is the necessity for those who have much to share with those who have little. The young mother explains to her children that this is not a story to document the existence of a place of perpetual torment—a place that contradicts God's love—but rather that the rich can be so preoccupied with what they have that they separate themselves from greater riches—the joy of responding to the needs of others.

Then the young mother can read to her children the creation accounts in Genesis (1:1-31; 2:1—3:24). Through the interpretive lens of love, she explains the wonders and goodness of creation and the endless possibilities for all. She explains that the reading is far less about how the world was made long ago and far more about how it is today. The introduction of evil opens the door for talking about sin—the lack of love—and how we can hurt ourselves and one another when we always put ourselves above our sisters and brothers.

As a lens for the reading of the Bible, she can read to the children the Great Commandment: "You shall love the Lord your God with all your heart and with all your soul and with all your mind; and your neighbor as yourself." Not only does this passage summarize holy scripture as God's love story with creation, but it also introduces the centrality of the soul as a part of humanity. This mother can explain that each of her children, and indeed all of us, have the gift of souls. She can explain that we all are made in the divine image and therefore have a spiritual birthright that complements the heart and mind. She can tell them that the spiritual power and guidance for all creation is Christ, who came to us long ago as Jesus to reveal more fully the very nature of the divine.

But there's more. This young mother has grown in spiritual treasure and soul development, giving her the ability to interpret scripture through love. Through Christian formation, she has begun her pilgrimage in faith. In worship this is reinforced because clergy who are nurtured through this kind of formation begin preaching with a focus on the soul, the development of spiritual treasure, and Christ as spiritual power and guidance. This young mother and those worshiping with her enjoy the music, not only for the beauty of the voices but also for the penetrating words of the hymn. Because of a stronger spirituality, even the architecture and stained glass of the church nurture their faith. In all these ways the Bible is reclaimed because its primary message of divine love has been underlined, lifted up, amplified, and heard.

REFLECT AND RESPOND

* Have you ever considered biblical interpretation through love as a possibility? Does it make sense to you?

* Do you think there is need for a more comprehensive way to use scripture? Why?

* Do you think interpretation of scripture through love could be effective in dealing with explosive issues?

* What is your comfort level of using the biblical history of adaptation to new discovery and changing circumstances for your own faith journey? For explaining scripture to others?

* What do you think about responding to secular cultural change with a mission to leaven it as contrasted with viewing secular culture as so often detrimental to or opposed to faith?

* Does your faith tradition act as if it has a monopoly on God, with God not operative beyond it? Is this silently assumed?

CHAPTER 5
RECLAIMING **THE MISSIONARY CALL**

Because of heightened uncertainty globally, people today within the church and those beyond tend to be more fearful, isolated, confused, and anxious. The old hymn "Just As I Am, Without One Plea" by Charlotte Elliott defines the human condition and longing well:

Just as I am, though tossed about,
With many a conflict, many a doubt
Fightings and fears, within, without,
O Lamb of God, I come, I come.

This creates an enormous opportunity for a church to address deeper human needs that are denied by our surrounding secular society. The church should take secular society up on its (sometimes implicit) dare and show how souls are fed and nurtured for living a fuller, deeper life.

As mentioned in Chapter 1, this opportunity has led Presiding Bishop Michael B. Curry to challenge the Episcopal Church to become part of the Jesus Movement. This vision is high and holy, and I hope it will be embraced by Episcopalians and Christians from other traditions as well. How better could it be implemented than by locally forming disciples who are equipped to pursue the holy goals of the Jesus Movement? How better could these local disciples be equipped than with a strong, robust spirituality that enables them through divine power and guidance to "do more than you can ask or imagine" (Ephesians 3:20-21)? What better approach could be taken than with a spiritually empowered missionary effort that lifts up mutual respect as a core value and calls for a loving and respectful evangelism? The local Christian formation process outlined in Chapter 2 establishes this model in which the church can call for and pursue equipping the spiritually hungry, inspiring them to use their spirituality to reach outward to others who have the same spiritual hunger. In a word, a synonym for a missionary church would be a serving church. It would be a community of miraculous expectation that is passionate about creating a healthier, more stable, and more just society.

At a time when churches of all kinds are struggling to adjust to the enormous cultural shifts of the twenty-first century, the missionary challenge is to offer a beautiful, powerful, and lasting counterbalance to those ever-constant pressures that degrade human life. The missionary call is to serve people by helping them get in touch with their souls and to live into the spiritual potential that is theirs through their birthright.

THE MIND OF A MISSIONARY

The task of the missionary church is to save souls. But this begs the questions: What are we saving souls for? And from what? Much New Testament rhetoric views saving souls as survival in the face of an immediately expected reordering of the cosmos. In other words, you need your soul saved so that when Jesus returns, you'll be ready. When the return of Christ wasn't immediate, the faithful adapted their expectation of salvation to the assurance of eternal life—and escape from the torments of hell—and many came to believe eternal life would be granted only to the baptized. A higher understanding of missionary call is based on a mutual respect that unfolds beautifully when love is affirmed as the primary divine mandate. With God in Christ as sovereign of all—sovereign even over hell—salvation becomes rescue from the demonic in life for both present and into eternity, saving individuals from their baser selves and challenging them to use their spiritual wealth and ingenuity to create a healthier society. Judgment is left in God's hands.

The goal, then, of evangelism—of enabling people to discover, and claim, their spiritual birthright as children of a God who created and sustains them and all creation with love—is the conversion of individuals so more people will work for a better, holier, and more just society. Evangelists and missionaries are the shock troops that implement the charge in the Lord's Prayer: "Thy kingdom come, thy will be done, on earth as it is in heaven." The reward is a fulfilling pilgrimage through this life and all that lies beyond.

The missionary is committed to a comprehensive, high vision of Christ—what theologians call a high Christology (that is, a high teaching about who Christ is). Such a Christology begins by remembering that while the world did not know Christianity as such before the time of Jesus, scripture assures us that Christ has always been present in the whole of creation, because Jesus is the Christian vision of God. When Jesus says he is "the way, and the truth, and the life. No one comes to the Father except through me," Christ is explaining that he is the divine source, whether known by others as such or not (John 14:6). This makes it possible to affirm, respect, and accommodate all sorts and conditions of peoples, religions, and those with no religion at all. Salvation by any definition is divine in origin or, in Christian terminology, by grace. All that is divine is in Christ, whether the source is recognized or not, whether Christian or otherwise.

The missionary mindset understands that Christ is not limited to the Church. Although Jesus as Christ has always existed from the time of creation, the Bible clearly affirms that no community of faith has a monopoly on the divine. Christ works everywhere and potentially with all. The three wise men were not Jews. Neither was Cyrus the Persian King, who initiated the return of the Hebrew exiles to the Land of Promise. Rahab the Harlot was neither Jewish nor an exemplary character, yet she was the divine choice to aid Joshua's spies. The entire book of Jonah is a testimony of the divine interest in a heathen city. In that book, Jonah was delighted to be blessed by the divine but fought with his life to keep that divine goodness from being extended. Moses was saved as a baby by Pharaoh's daughter. Naaman the Syrian came to Elisha the prophet in Israel for healing. So clearly God is active beyond "the chosen." Jesus said he had sheep "that do not belong to this fold" (John 10:16). In the parable of the Last Judgment, it was those who had acted in love to help those in need who were ultimately rewarded (Matthew 25:31-46). Saint Paul writes that creation itself reveals the divine. "Ever since the creation of the world his eternal power and divine nature, invisible though they are, have been understood and seen through the things he has made" (Romans 1:20).

So mutual respect relieves Christians of the enormous burden of thinking that all must become Christian to be within the divine orbit. The scope and creative energy of the missionary is then freed to build discipleship and help people live more productively. Since all must ultimately come before the judgment seat of Christ, the missionary does not judge on the basis of another's religion or lack thereof. The missionary does not deny hell. Yes, the Bible does indeed reference a hell of torment and it testifies to a God who gets angry and acts wrathfully. Yet the same scripture unfolds around a loving God, one who is always capable of forgiveness, one who says, "for I will forgive their iniquity, and remember their sin no more" (Jeremiah 31:34). So the missionary task is to nurture souls and encourage them to experience Christ as the high road of life, to expect eternal life and leave the eternal destiny of others in divine hands.

All of this means that instead of believing that Christianity has surrendered to culture, the church's missionary call is to enrich and leaven culture as it grapples with new discovery and ever-changing circumstances. The missionary call seeks to challenge self-serving people who are suspicious, indifferent, and sometimes hostile to religion. The missionary call fosters an evangelism centered on serving from a posture of affirming the good that is in people; it gives direction and spiritual resources to bolster individuals' better instincts, so they can use their resources to attack the darker side of life.

The missionary call seeks those who hunger for something better and hopeful. They are the lonely, strugglers of all kinds, refugees from bad church or religious experiences, those who seek a better way of life, religious skeptics, and those sensing something is missing in their lives. The audience includes those looking for love, human connection, greater purpose, and personal or professional fulfillment. This audience wants resources to deal with all the manifestations of evil. They crave a deep inner strength, mercy when needed, guidance when lost, help when perplexed, and inspiration to attain the deeper joys of life. They are the mission field—and as Jesus said, "The harvest is plentiful" (Luke 10:2). And then he also said: "Come to me, all you that are weary and are carrying heavy burdens, and I will give you rest" (Matthew 11:28).

This mindset recognizes the awesome potential of a missionary team. The broader missionary team includes church members who are in touch with their spiritual wealth and can articulate it. They are dedicated church members who consider it a privilege to invite potential newcomers into a sphere of the church's mission and ministry. The congregation's inviters are then complemented by a trained and commissioned formation team to engage in more depth the riches of Christianity.

Most fundamentally, the missionary mindset is shaped by what Jesus said and did. He came to connect people to their deeper and fuller selves, to rescue them from their baser and more narrow concepts of life. He came to make them whole. He came to emancipate them from the erroneous idea that material acquisitions and unhealthy influence over others will satisfy deep human yearnings.

Humility was central to Jesus and his missionary identity. He was born in a humble setting, to humble parents. He lived in a humble way. His humility was his strength, even as his strength enabled him to be humble. Coming to serve and not to be served, he did not overpower. By refusing to use his power to change a political or a religious system, Jesus claimed for himself and for his followers a kingdom not governed by worldly wisdom or human establishment. As such his power was made perfect by weakness, yet with an underlying strength that could not be held in check by human authority or manipulation. Such humility makes the missionary call of today even more attractive and powerful.

Thomas Tallis's hymn, "The Great Creator of the Worlds," written around 1567, is built on this theological base, especially in its closing stanzas:

He came as Savior to his own, the way of love he trod;
He came to win men by good will, for force is not
of God.
Not to oppress, but summon men, their truest life
to find,
In love God sent his Son to save, not to condemn
mankind.

The missionary call is to be proclaimed from a posture of humility, a motivation to serve, an eagerness to engage, and with a repository of spiritual treasure.

Jesus, the first missionary of Christianity, arrived as the Incarnation—"Jesus, the pioneer and perfecter of our faith, who for the sake of the joy that was set before him endured the cross" (Hebrews 12:2). His reward was joy. What a joy it must have been to see people regain hope, to realize there was a power beyond ordinary prediction to counteract the drudgery, inequality, and brutality of life. The joy of seeing the lame walk, the blind see, and the hungry fed. The joy of exposing a kingdom in this world not bound by the forces that enslave or degrade. The joy of possessing a power that could make a difference, could elevate lives, and create a higher vision. The joy of seeing happiness and relief in those who need a love that affirmed their value and worth. That same promise of joy is the reward today for those who give themselves in a missionary way.

The missionary knows that God is always at work. Everywhere. Where you, the reader, live and serve. The missionary knows that the essentials of Christianity never change. Spiritual wealth— power and guidance for an abundant life lived in harmony with the divine—is the most potent asset of the church. And because those with a missionary mindset recognize human sin as rebellion against this divine source, disciples are cognizant of their continual need of forgiveness. Spiritual treasure is a counterbalance to the demonic forces of the universe and a source of hope. It led the peoples of the Bible through their trials and struggles. This magnificent treasure was and is gained through encounter with Christ, whether directly or through others or special events. It accumulates with time. It fulfills what Saint Paul writes, "Even though our outer nature is wasting away, our inner nature is being renewed day by day" (2 Corinthians 4:16).

The basic components of Christianity for missionary engagement are in place—proclamation, preaching, worship, sacraments, scripture, faith, music, teaching, service, the creeds, and the Christian year. The congregation that wants to move into a more effective missionary posture continues this work—but with key adaptations about *how* they are doing worship and music, service and formation. Often churches without strong spiritual formation ministries are doing the right things, but with too modest an aim and inadequate gospel transmission. That is, too often, churches preach and celebrate the eucharist and sing simply to maintain or to grow the church as church. Maintaining or even growing the church is not our mission. Helping God save souls from lives of narrowness is our mission. Introducing people to the Christian way of life and helping them live into that life, using their inner strength to reach outward, is our mission.

THE MISSIONARY APPROACH

People with a missionary mindset will not lapse into thinking, "I've got something to share or tell, and without it you will continue to be lost and beyond God's help." Rather, their approach will be, "I've discovered something of the divine that has enriched my life, and maybe you are seeking the same. If you want, let's explore this together." This is the way of love, not with force or veiled intimidation but with humility and a desire to help others find their truer selves.

To love another requires the one offering love to know the needs of others. Yes, they need Christ. Yet isn't Christ more real to newcomers when they experience someone interested in their more immediate longings? In thinking about this, I am influenced by Abraham Maslow's famous "Hierarchy of Needs," which argues that a person who is focused on meeting basic needs for food, water, shelter, and immediate safety cannot worry about meeting needs like achievement, beauty, significance, meaning, inner potential, and morality. A person who hasn't eaten in two days is not going to be able to listen with much attention to an evangelistic pitch—that's obvious enough. But equally true is the idea that a person who is in search of a life partner or who is scared of being fired will likely be more receptive to hearing about God from someone who has taken the time to know about these life struggles. Otherwise, the evangelistic intentions may seem little more than dispensing tracts.

The need for love and belonging are ever present, and members of the household of faith should recognize this in every person, member, or newcomer who steps onto church property. Likewise all need esteem. Being told all are made in God's image helps, but more imporant is being treated, within a community of faith, as one who bears God's image. People's quests for significance, beauty, achievement, meaning, and justice are deepened and enriched when we see our desire for these is itself a gift from the God who made them and us.

Each tradition of Christianity has an opportunity to articulate its vision of living into the divine command to love. Speaking as only one bishop and certainly not on behalf of the entire Episcopal Church, I offer in my own words a comprehensive

Christian missionary approach that assumes that every religion has as a purpose the blessing of people through a divine source. Therefore with regard to missionary posture, a missionary:

◆ Respects Christians from other denominations and does not proselytize their active members

◆ Respects those of other religions and does not convert their active adherents

◆ Seeks to share Christ as the source of all spiritual treasure with all who come as seekers, yet in a way that helps them in their individual life situations

◆ Does not consider proselytizing as reaching out to seekers who are no longer active in any faith community

This posture assumes a servant posture to evangelism, humble in approaching others and with a desire for people to grow in love. It respects all. I have often felt it especially imperative to practice this kind of missionary mindset at Episcopal schools, where I've been privileged to lead worship and preach. Episcopal schools are interesting microcosms of the larger society—while there are certainly some Episcopalians, the student body usually includes many Christians from other traditions as well as non-Christians. When approaching these chapel services and the question of whether and how non-Christians should participate, I have used the following guidelines, which I hope reflect the missionary mindset I've laid out in this chapter:

◆ Non-Christians are encouraged to live into the higher calling of their faith and to use Episcopal worship as an educational and spiritual means of learning more about the Christian faith

- Non-Episcopal Christians can use the experience to foster a better understanding of their own faith tradition and can use the experience to deepen their understanding of the Episcopal Church.

- Those of no religion can use the experience as educational to know more about the Christian faith as practiced by the Episcopal Church and possibly to become a part of it

- The entire worship offering should be an exercise in toleration and respect for all religions and those with no religious tradition

Such an approach honors all and offers a high vision of mutual respect for a world torn in so many ways by religious division. At the same time, my approach, I hope, takes seriously the sincere belief of the Christian church that those without God live narrower lives than those who know God.

ENGAGING THE MISSION FIELD

One of the biddings in *The Book of Common Prayer* says, "I ask your prayers for all who seek God, or a deeper knowledge of him" (386). When I say this, I remind you that most people in the world have this desire for deeper knowledge of God. This is not surprising as humans are created in the image of the creator and are spiritual by nature. The missionary call of Christ is an effort to address this universal human yearning. The missionary call leads to engagement of those who could become Christians. Making church members is so often the stated goal—and spirituality is considered that goal's handmaiden, which is, of course, backwards. The real goal is to offer spiritual growth to people and to invite people to worship God; it should not be assumed that spiritual growth automatically happens when someone joins a church. Rather, churches need to intentionally and explicitly pursue the spiritual development of all people, inviting those outside into this quest. Acceptance of Christ is only the first step, a birth into the Christian community of miraculous expectation, from which life will continue to grow throughout an earthly pilgrimage and into eternity.

The approach is invitational. Yet even before an invitation, a relationship is needed. When the invitation becomes for something more than "church," it is more likely to appeal to the hearer's need. Church as church is not altogether attractive to many. To some it is actually a put-off. To assist inviters with a more helpful invitation, the Church of the Heavenly Rest has developed a calling card with a picture of its facilities on one side along with the words, "Building up Spiritual Treasure." The card directs recipients' attention to what a newcomer would be offered, namely spiritual development upon which a person builds.

Invitations to a church potluck, worship service, or book study meeting—all should be offered as acts of love, regardless of the response. An invitation communicates that the one invited has value. The unspoken message from the inviter to the one being invited is, "I live a life of faith in which I find value. I have a spiritual community where that value is enhanced. I am open to sharing what I value with you if you are seeking something similar." If the listener declines, one hopes both the listener and the one who invited her will feel a sense of ease and feel no pressure or judgment. If the listener is already of another faith or tradition and thus not seeking, the inviter can acknowledge and affirm that. But to the one who feels unattached and is seeking, the invitation becomes a potential pathway to greater health and a fuller life.

It is essential to remember that before beginning a missionary endeavor, a congregation should undertake a self-audit, a congregational self-evaluation. A prerequisite for missionary work is health. There must be bonds of trust with clergy and laity. Good, working relationships among the nucleus of the congregation ensure that those coming into the congregation find a healthy, wholesome place. If the audit reveals inner disharmony and excessive strife, the congregation's first task is to get well.

For those with congregational health, the missionary call of Christ calls for interfacing with others. A splendidly effective implementation for this is called *Invite Welcome Connect,* developed by Mary Parmer. This ministry follows simple organizational principles by encouraging all in a congregation to invite people to church events and/or outreach ministries and provides a methodology to aid this.

As part of the Invite Welcome Connect initiative, congregations form a welcome team to identify and engage newcomers. Those who express interest are invited to delve into the basics of Christianity. For those who do become church members, another team helps integrate them into the ministry of the congregation. A growing number of Episcopal congregations are using this approach with remarkable success. Small wonder, for it is based on love and as such presents an organizational way for the faithful to love those who are potential newcomers. Following are stories of several congregations using this missionary approach.

Christ Episcopal Cathedral in Lexington, Kentucky, uses this ministry initiative. The Very Rev. Carol Wade, dean, and the Rev. Canon Brent Owens, an associate, report a 28 percent increase in membership from 2010 to 2015—that is, membership increased from 957 to 1,222. Their average Sunday attendance

(ASA) has increased from 337 to 564 during the same period, an increase of 67 percent. Welcome and invite teams are as much a part of congregational life as the choir. The welcome team was formed first and now has thirty-seven greeters. An invite team has been created and the connect team is planned. A fourth Sunday service has been added. They've instituted a monthly Sunday afternoon Evensong (choral service). A "Seven Marks of Membership" gives newcomers what is expected of them should they become a part of this outpost for mission in Lexington; it creates a clear pathway for spiritual growth and discipleship that provides support to their new life in Christ.

Another church utilizing the *Invite Welcome Connect* ministry began with an inventory. Hillary Raining, rector of St. Christopher's Episcopal Church in Gladwyne, Pennsylvania, writes:

Gladwyne is a suburb of Philadelphia. The parish itself was founded in the baby-boom of post-WWII America. Like so many churches that started in that era, our numbers have declined over the years. Some of that decline is due to a drop in local population and the reality of decreased church attendance in the general public, as well as a somewhat undefined Christian identity.

When I arrived as rector, our vestry looked at our community in a holistic approach, starting with our very mission. While the mission statement at that time— "to provide a thoughtful and active community of faith, fellowship, and ministry"—pointed to some clear truths about our church, it failed to have a charge to action. It also left out any mention of God. Thus, a new mission statement was discerned: "To lift people up as Christ calls." This statement combined what we already loved about this place—that we do lift each other up in times of joy and need—gave us an active call to seek new people and ways to lift up all things—our hearts, our talents, our needs, our treasures, etc.—to God as Christ calls.

Raining and lay leaders saw the necessity of getting more focused on Christ as a prerequisite for any other type of growth.

We engaged in a program called *RenewalWorks*, which is a catalyst for refocusing parishes (and the individuals in them) on spiritual vitality. A ministry of Forward Movement, the *RenewalWorks* process began with an anonymous, confidential, online inventory taken by our congregants, exploring that individual's spiritual life. When the responses were viewed as a group, the inventory provided a snapshot of the spiritual vitality of the congregation. The data revealed some areas of strengths (such as a deep love and care for each other and a desire to welcome everyone) and some areas of growth (such as a need to expand our knowledge of the Bible and spiritual practices).

The ability to spend some time growing in our Christian identity and faith has meant that people are more excited about their church and are more likely to invite people to join. They are creative and willing to try new things. They have found that they love reading the Bible and learning more about our Christian faith. I feel so blessed to be a part of this community and experience them growing—not just in numbers—but in the Holy Spirit.

A final story regarding those who use the *Invite Welcome Connect* ministry model comes from St. John's Episcopal Church in Tallahassee, Florida. The Rev. David Killeen, rector, writes:

In 2005, led by the rector, half the parish and almost the entire staff left St. John's to form another church in Tallahassee. This was a traumatic event for the church and the community. It wasn't strangers who left, but siblings, coworkers, colleagues, and friends. After years of difficult transition, I was called as priest-in-charge and then rector. I focused on leading a comprehensive effort of parish-wide discernment of core values, mission, vision, as well as specific strategies and goals. More than 300 lay members of all ages, including youth, came together over the course of a year to listen for God's dream for St. John's.

Goal #1 of the strategic plan spotlighted the importance of Christian formation as central to congregational growth and vitality. Regarding new member catechesis and formation, we put a lot of energy into the *Invite Welcome Connect* approach. *Connect*, in particular, is where our Christian formation has an impact. We offer new members' classes four to five times a year. We share our spiritual journeys, take a historical tour of the campus, and learn about the full arc of salvation history as well as discuss the history of the church and teach about Christian stewardship of time, talent, and treasure. New members can also take a "deeper dive" in Growing in Grace, our three-month class for those seeking adult confirmation of preparation for adult baptism. Here, we examine in greater detail the core teachings of the church. The class, which typically involves around thirty adults, involves lecture-style presentations, small group discussions, a Saturday full-day retreat at the beach, and a service project.

In the last seven years, St. John's average Sunday attendance has grown from 360 to 460, 28 percent growth. Our financial giving is up by approximately the same amount, and we just completed a $5 million capital campaign to complete historic preservation work on the church and build a new welcome center.

All of these congregations are expanding their Christian formation efforts, and I believe they are right on target with their objectives. They realize that their growth in number, exciting as it is, will perpetuate a weakened church if a good spiritual foundation is not in place. So they've made spiritual nurture the heart of their invitation to newcomers and long-time members alike.

Some churches offer spiritual practices that are not explicitly Christian but feed and nurture the spiritual life. These congregations attract the spiritually hungry and bring them into an environment from which they could come into the church. An example comes from Christ Episcopal Cathedral in Houston. The church opened the Hines Center for Spirituality and Prayer in 2015. Located in a building across from the cathedral in the heart of downtown Houston, the center offers yoga in a whole host of expressions, dance, Tai Ji (Tai Chi), centering prayer, meditation, meditation movement, and a book study. The Very Rev. Barkley Thompson, cathedral dean, and his leadership team discovered some interesting data about spiritual practices among their own membership. They found that members use a variety of techniques beyond those offered only in church as a way to build their spiritual treasure.

The survey found:

- 64 percent actively pursue spirituality outside of traditional church confines

- ◆ 83 percent engage in practices outside of traditional worship and prayer to strengthen their connection to God

- ◆ 89 percent believe there are practices outside of traditional worship and prayer that strengthen their connection to God

- ◆ 85 percent appreciate alternative spiritual practices that provide others with positive spiritual benefits

- ◆ 85 percent are interested in learning about ancient spiritual practices

- ◆ 72 percent have experienced meditation and the vast majority report that meditation has benefited them spiritually and wish they could practice it through the church

- ◆ 75 percent agreed with the statement, "Taking part in interfaith discussions can improve my relationship with God." Of those, 90 percent stated that they would be interested in taking part in interfaith programming through the church

The Hines Center is a brilliant strategic response to the realities revealed by the survey. The center supports Christ Church parishioners by providing access to techniques that raise spiritual awareness and support the growth of their spiritual treasure. It is also an opportunity for non-church members to be in contact with parishioners, to see their joy in Christ, and perhaps to consider attending the church.

FINAL THOUGHTS

This presentation and understanding of a missionary theology is offered in love and concern. Growth comes through challenge. A large component of the opportunity at-hand is a willingness on the part of those who care deeply about the church to lay aside disagreements and instead glean what appears to offer health and hope. Repeating what Gamaliel said, what is of the Holy Spirit will prevail. What isn't will not last.

In the twenty-first century we are moving into a completely new world order and it is time to adapt to its needs. This passage from Ecclesiastes 3:1-3 has been helpful to me in praying for guidance and understanding and adapting my own scope of call. Part of it reads:

> For everything there is a season, and a time for every
>   matter under heaven:
> a time to be born, and a time to die;
> a time to plant, and a time to pluck up what is planted;
> a time to kill, and a time to heal;
> a time to break down, and a time to build up.

The present is a time to build up, regroup, re-access, refocus, and reclaim.

REFLECT AND RESPOND

- ♦ How should Christians think about other religions?

- ♦ Should Christians try to convert active members of other faith traditions? Do you or your church try to do so?

- ♦ Does mutual respect have a place in the face of divisive issues that challenge practices and beliefs that Christians have long held?

- ♦ In your mind what is church growth—adding new members? Anything beyond? How would you know if your church had grown?

- ♦ Does your congregation's approach to missionary call do anything significant to reverse the decline of Christianity? To reverse the growth of those who claim to be spiritual but not religious?

- ♦ To what degree is missionary call a method to strengthen the congregation? To what extent is it to the strengthen individuals spiritually?

CHAPTER 6
RECLAIMING **A CULTURE OF HOPE**

Clergy yearn inwardly for a working place that offers hope the gospel promises, that unites them with each other in mission, that nurtures their souls as they minister to others, that enables them to lead in the miraculous transformation of lives and gives them cause for celebration when they come together. They also yearn for a church equipped to influence both individuals and community in a significant way. This chapter documents an Episcopal Church movement that is enabling clergy to break individual isolation, minimize competitiveness among themselves, and find spiritual strength and direction. The movement is dedicated to the renewal of Christianity and has become a research and development team within the Episcopal Church.

Known as the Gathering of Leaders, learnings from its scope and structure have been a primary resource for our first five chapters. What follows is the story of the Gathering's founding, its vision, mission, core values, and structure, and the reasons for its effectiveness. The bottom line is this: the Gathering has strengthened clergy through immersion into a church culture and structure of affirmation and hope, and it has inspired and guided them to renew places they serve and far beyond. While the whys and how-tos are Episcopal in origin, they are apropos for any Christian body. And while this chapter focuses on a movement designed to aid entrepreneurial clergy, learnings from their work are highly germane for any congregation or other church entity.

In the summer of 2004, two Episcopalians were enjoying lunch in southwestern Wyoming after a morning round of golf. Conversation gravitated toward the dismal state of the Episcopal Church, not only from its general decline but also over the internal havoc caused by the church's decision a year earlier to consecrate an openly gay man as a bishop. These two leaders discussed various church needs and then wondered whether they could do anything helpful. Considering this for about a year, they called on others to ponder possibilities.

I was one of those two leaders. John Castle, a prominent attorney in Dallas, was the other. We met in 2000, when I was bishop of the Episcopal Diocese of Texas. We quickly realized that we had a shared passion: We were Episcopalians who wanted to serve those beyond the church. Like me, John believed that Jesus had come to transform lives through spiritual power and guidance, and he wanted the church to identify as a community of miraculous expectation, with each congregation self-identifying as a missionary outpost.

This missionary vision I shared with John assumed the entire diocese to be one single church, united in mission, rather than congregations and institutions separately doing some version of their own vision. So John and I had been friends for several years when we had our conversation, which eventually gave rise to the Gathering of Leaders.

As you read about this movement and some of its results, keep in mind the concepts of team and peer engagement. As a team of two peers, John and I began by inviting some thirty church leaders, mostly clergy, from across the United States, to explore a way forward for Christian renewal. Entrepreneurially experienced bishops, priests, and lay persons made up the mix of people, carefully selected because all points of view on the highly explosive issue of sexuality, as well as gender and racial diversity, had to be present to command respect throughout the Episcopal Church. We wanted our group to be known for a commitment to a vision of the renewal of the Christian faith in the Episcopal Church in the face of conflict and decline, not for a particular view on sexuality. Some twenty-two invitees responded for a two-day meeting. We bonded because each of us brought a deep desire for recovery, recognition of a need for structure for accomplishment, and realization that core values would dictate our behavior and outlook. The result was the beginning of a healthy, hopeful, and beautiful culture among ourselves that we would perpetuate and expand.

We named ourselves The Gathering of Leaders. We decided to organize our time together around "Gatherings," where invitees could share the good things occurring in places where they serve. We established and refined our process over the years. Today, the Gathering is primarily for clergy, with attendance limited to forty to maximize peer engagement. Invitees are selected from those deemed best qualified for the intended result: namely clergy giving leadership that is producing growth in some form. Though not so named as such, the Gathering of Leaders participants have become an ad hoc, non-institutional research and development team for the Episcopal Church in search of ways for Christian recovery. They share success stories. They exchange ideas. They reveal new discoveries. Since the first Gathering in 2006 through some forty others since, more than five hundred clergy have taken part. At each Gathering, attendees nominate other clergy they know who fit the criteria of showing growth where they serve. Once you attend, you remain on the invitation list for all Gatherings. At any one Gathering, both returning and new participants attend. Though they don't all know each other, many stay connected through social media and often expand their team connection and scope through attendance at more Gatherings.

Gatherings are scheduled from Monday afternoon until noon Wednesday at various times each year and at scattered locations. More than half of the participants are assigned leadership roles—for Bible study, worship, various presentations, subgroup facilitators—all focused on a vision of the recovery of Christianity through the church. Two lay facilitators run the meetings. Evenings are completely free of any scheduled events to maximize peer communication. There is no hierarchy— bishops, clergy, and lay persons share what they are doing that is working, what they have done that didn't work, and what they hope for the future. Participants sit at tables, with discussion after each presentation. Those in attendance move from table to table, during presentations and meals, so they can spend in-depth time with a variety of participants.

TESTIMONIALS SUPPORTING CORE VALUES

As part of this chapter about Reclaiming a Culture of Hope, I want to share several stories from participants of the Gathering of Leaders. Their stories are inspiring, giving hope to congregations large and small that growth of all kinds will come with faithfulness and with a commitment to listening and responding to the Holy Spirit. For the Rev. Luke Jernagan, rector of Saint Peter's Church, Saint Louis, Missouri, the Gathering of Leaders has spurred a "renewed excitement about who we are as an Episcopal Church." He writes:

> When I go to a Gathering, I feel real excitement and enthusiasm for what's happening within the church walls, and how lives are being transformed, and how people are engaging with the holy, deepening their relationship with God. In a time when people talk so much about the death of the church, here's a group of clergy who are experiencing the opposite.
>
> I know clergy who are competitive, and I don't get that sense in the Gathering of Leaders. I feel it's a group that genuinely wants to see each other do well. And that's the thing, it's all about the free sharing of ideas; to be able to say, "Hey, this is something that worked at our church, and here are the quantifiable results. I'm more than happy to help you start the same in your parish. I find, unfortunately, that this is rare among clergy.

Here is a member of the clergy who is hopeful, who sees green when others are seeing red, who is an example of dedication to a theology of abundance as contrasted to scarcity. It reflects the living out of what Saint Paul described when he wrote, "I can do all things through him who strengthens me" (Philippians 4:13). No evidence of isolation or competitiveness here.

Hope is a core value absolutely necessary to success with any endeavor to change culture. In the initial years of the Gathering of Leaders, a number of clergy, congregations, and even some dioceses were leaving the Episcopal Church. Consequently, hope for the Episcopal Church itself was an issue for many. As a testimony to hope found, the Rev. Morgan Allen, rector of the Episcopal Church of the Good Shepherd, Austin, Texas, says, "The Gathering of Leaders gives me hope in hope. That is, my Christian hope has been supported and strengthened by the hope I gain from witnessing the capacity and creativity of the Episcopal Church through its leaders at Gatherings. In my estimation this is no small achievement. In most seasons of my life, my Christian hope has been entirely a leap of faith, as I did not see much evidence that Jesus' decision to entrust to the church the salvation of the cosmos was a wise investment. However, the stories I hear at Gatherings give me hope in hope: that lives can and are being transformed in the name of Jesus Christ, and we don't have to wait until Jesus' return for that to happen."

Peer learning and engagement, resulting in the creation of ministry teams, is the core value that constitutes the means of engagement. "Upon entering my first Gathering," says the Rt. Rev. Daniel Gutierrez, who began attending Gatherings long before he became bishop of Pennsylvania. "I had the expectation of a routine clergy conference. My expectations were immediately and pleasantly dashed. I found a community of creativity, hope, and vision. Without a hint of arrogance and competition, I listened to peers sharing innovative ideas, cutting edge outreach, and growth strategies."

The Rev. Gar Demo, rector of the Church of St. Thomas the Apostle, Overland Park, Kansas, says, "I enjoyed the evening free hours to take a deep breath." He said that the time to socialize freely with other participants "gave an added dimension to my peer learning." And the Rev. Jimmy Bartz, then of Thad's, an emerging congregation in Los Angeles and now rector of St. John's, Jackson, Wyoming, says, "There's a secret sauce at these Gatherings. That's been very important to my ministry and has really added to my development as I deepen my priesthood within the kind of crazy, creative context in west Los Angeles."

When Episcopal Bishop Jeff Fisher was rector of St. Alban's Church, Waco, Texas, he used peer engagement and team formation he experienced at Gatherings to lead that congregation into a much-needed ministry adjustment. He writes:

> My story of resurrection leadership included how I had led the parish, in my first few months as rector, to close the parish school that had been a fixture in Waco for sixty years. The school had outlived its usefulness and was facing many challenges. Addressing the congregation, I said, "I am not afraid to re-imagine that empty school building as a place of resurrection."

> The old school building was resurrected as the St. Alban's Outreach Center, housing ministries to children, hosting four times as many children as when we operated a school. Not only was the building resurrected, but also the parish experienced unprecedented growth in membership, income, and attendance.

> To get there it was the team that made it all work. The outcome wasn't just the attainment of a new plan. How they used the crisis they faced as opportunity, and how they created a team to work together, created far more than a goal for facility use. It created a group with interconnecting relationships that enabled parishioners to share ideas, ask for divine guidance, speculate on plans, eat snacks and drink coffee together, and in the process feel more connected. In biblical imagery, they became a functioning body of Christ, not just individuals. The congregation grew in vision, morale, spirit, confidence,

participation, and health. Peer engagement essentially molded the entire congregation into a team to recognize the need for change and to search for and perfect a new and viable ministry utilizing what they already had, a school building.

The missionary call of Christ, which threads through each of these testimonies, is anchored in the belief that Christ both directs and empowers mission. It was very evident at Trinity Episcopal Church, Galveston, Texas, following the disaster of Hurricane Ike in 2008. Rector Susan Kennard writes:

I accepted a call to serve as priest-in-charge of Trinity, Galveston, in December of 2011. The parochial report for the year 2011 lists an average Sunday attendance of 128, divided between two Sunday services. The congregation had experienced a long period of decline, a long period of conflict, and a direct hit from Hurricane Ike in 2008. In a way, the storm was a defining moment. The faithful remaining members of Trinity rebuilt their own homes and their church home. They continued to support the church financially, and they survived.

I imagined that this small but historic congregation (meeting in a really big space) would be hesitant to welcome new leadership, hesitant to call a woman, hesitant to form relationships of trust. In fact, I had completely underestimated their tenacity and their great thirst for the Good News of Jesus Christ. They were so eager to hear words of hope and confidence, plans of hope and confidence, and sermons of hope and confidence that new, resurrected life began to happen at once.

This is a congregation that was ready to grow, and said things to me like, "Tell us what to do, and we will do it." Then they did. My vision for the renewed life and vitality of Trinity was not anything like rocket science: restore the nursery, hire nursery workers, think outside the box in Christian formation, excellence in preaching, excellence in worship, train some acolytes, get kids to the diocesan mission trip, get out there in the community and make some new friends. On Ash Wednesday we started "Ashes to Go" on the seawall and the first year anointed over a hundred people, including a bus-full from a local head injury recovery center. We started having an Easter Vigil down on the beach, and the first year baptized seven people. We started a small service on Sunday evenings, *Come As You Are*, and anywhere from fifteen to twenty people are coming. As we submitted to the diocese the parochial report for 2015, our average Sunday attendance is 179. This is a small number for many congregations, but for us, it's an increase of 40 percent in four years. We are alive. The spirit of our community is alive and has grown in ways that are immeasurable as we have added new members and programs, and as existing members and programs have been healed by the Spirit of Jesus.

I am not ashamed or embarrassed to be counting those attendance numbers and keeping a running average all year long! (My parishioners are very familiar with my calculator and the service register all dog-eared from looking back at last year, last Christmas, etc.) ASA (average Sunday attendance) is not everything, but it is something, and it helps us to see where we have been, where we are going, and if we need to change some things along the pathway that we have chosen. What an amazing time to dedicate ourselves to the service of the living God, and to his son, Jesus Christ.

Mutual respect, another core value, was the backdrop to the amazing story of The Falls Church Episcopal in Falls Church, Virginia. Present rector John Ohmer shares the story:

In the mid to late 1980s, The Falls Church went through a period of massive numerical growth. During this time, its leadership began expressing increasingly strident opposition to the wider Episcopal Church, particularly around the issue of the full inclusion of gays and lesbians in all aspects of church life and its policy of allowing women to become bishops.

In 2006, the vast majority voted to leave the Episcopal Church, with only a hundred or so members remaining. Meanwhile, the several thousand departing congregants (now calling themselves The Falls Church Anglican) attempted to make a legal case that they were entitled to remain in possession of the buildings and grounds. In 2012, the Virginia Supreme Court unanimously ruled against The Falls Church Anglican. That decision required the departing group to leave the property. I joined this continuing congregation in 2012. The remnant small group returned to a sanctuary that seats well over 900. So as I joined this family-to-pastoral sized congregation of about 120 on a Sunday, we had some giants to face. One was financial pressure. We survived those first few years thanks to assistance from the Diocese of Virginia and neighboring Episcopal churches. They invested in us, believed in us, and worked with us because they believed in our potential.

Thanks to the prayer and hard work, and inspired by insights from the Gathering of Leaders, we completed a three-to-five-year vision process, stating five visions, or directions we believe we were called to go. Has it been working? Since returning to the property, we've seen attendance grow from an average of 120 on a Sunday to frequently over 300. We still maintain a sense of community, intimacy, and familiarity—but this is encouraging and sustainable growth.

We've let the wider community know we are here to serve, and there's hardly ever an evening that our facilities are not in use by some local organization. We transformed what was once a tape library and bookstore into a food pantry and have formed new partnerships with those serving the homeless and prisoners in our area, and the poor around the world. All that growth is good, but the most important growth we see is our members' growth in faith, hope, and love. The best and most encouraging growth is when someone is touched by God through their involvement in this church, and that touch makes them more faithful, more hopeful, and more loving in their everyday life. Glory to God, whose power working in us can do infinitely more than we can ask or imagine!

Rising from a setting where mutual respect was absent, this story illustrates how those practicing mutual respect bonded into a community of miraculous expectation.

Growth is another Gathering of Leaders' core value. This growth is defined in many ways, from regaining health and building trust to spiritual growth. The next stories show growth in various ways, including numbers, because their leaders have made this an expectation based on a renewed focus on Christ.

The Rev. Alison Harrity, rector of Saint Richard's, Winter Park, Florida, writes:

> My church is growing. After serving eleven years as an assistant in two large churches, I now work at a small church that had just over a hundred people on Sunday morning. In my first year, we grew 26 percent, and in my second year we grew 10.5 percent in our average Sunday attendance. While we added programs, a Sunday School, and outreach ministries, there is no gimmick or hook that has caused growth. More than anything, as I have learned from the Gathering of Leaders over the last six years, growth comes when leadership is focused on one thing: God. God is mercy, God is love. God is compassion, and God is acceptance. It reminds me every year that I am not alone, that God's work is never done, and that it can change lives and the whole world.

Another Gathering of Leaders' participant, the Rev. Rob Fisher serves as rector of St. Dunstan's in Carmel Valley, California. "We are a growing pastoral-sized church heading toward program size. It's a very energetic and active parish, 40 percent larger than it was when I arrived five and a half years ago. We have a ministry in Haiti supporting a sister parish and school of 1,200 kids. We raise $90,000 outside of our budget to support that ministry every year." By reaching outward, this church has grown in number driven by the spiritual growth of missionary call, anchored in hope, exercising mutual respect, and faithfully engaged in mission beyond themselves.

Another story of growth is the Diocese of Oklahoma. In 2007 the Rev. Ed Konieczny was elected bishop of Oklahoma. Attending his first Gathering, he met the Rev. José McLaughlin, who shortly afterward became his canon. They and others became a team concentrating on growth and development strategies, a vision for recruiting for candidates for ordination, and clergy recruitment following the thrust of the Gathering of Leaders. Some faltering congregations were restarted. Entrepreneurial clergy were sent to Gatherings. The diocese provided resources for congregational development. A land banking initiative was established to secure land for new churches. Growth by leadership, vision, and infrastructure came after four years of preparation. During the years 2012–2015, the entire diocese grew 4.3 percent in number, becoming one of the few in the Episcopal Church to record any growth. Their restart congregations are doing very well. In 2016, Canon McLaughlin was elected bishop of Western North Carolina. Networks have formed among diocesan clergy and now extend churchwide.

A final story comes from how the Gathering of Leaders has influenced the Episcopal Church's governing body through its participants. At the 2015 General Convention of the Episcopal Church, the Rev. Canon Scott Gunn, executive director of Forward Movement, worked with several clergy and lay leaders to petition the convention to redirect $3 million to fund the planting of new congregations. He reports,

> A couple of months before the convention, several friends and I met to craft a set of resolutions to implement a church vision of discipleship as contrasted to maintenance, of evangelism rather than preservation. Most of us who signed on what came to be called the Episcopal Resurrection Memorial knew each other through the Gathering of Leaders. Simply put, I do

not think we would have come together without the Gathering of Leaders. This is, I think, exactly the vision that Bishop Payne and John Castle set out to do. Over the years I've been taking part, I've met many fantastic leaders. As we seek to transform our church, whether locally or globally, this ministry will benefit from the invaluable network of the Gathering of Leaders.

Resolutions initiated by Gunn and his colleagues that included funding for new church plants and for training leaders were passed at this convention. The resolutions emphasized evangelism. At that same convention Bishop Michael B. Curry was elected as the Episcopal Church's presiding officer. Immediately he advocated that the Episcopal Church become a Jesus Movement with a threefold vision of reconciliation, care of creation, and evangelism.

LEARNINGS

The Gathering of Leaders is fulfilling its research and development effort to renew Christianity in the Episcopal Church. Learnings from this movement have shaped my understanding of the model of Christian formation presented in this book. This peer-engaged, spiritually centered team approach can also be used with groups other than Christian formation. Outreach projects, music ministries, youth ministries, ushers and greeters, and every conceivable subgroup in a congregation can use peer learning. New teams and existing ones can be deepened and strengthened by structuring times for faith stories and highlighting spiritual treasure.

For instance, ushers, already a team that hands out worship bulletins and takes up offerings, can meet together, share stories of faith with one another, expand their vision of purpose, and raise the level of love through the jobs they faithfully do week by week. In their meetings—scheduled periodically during the year—they train new ushers. They begin to discover more fully their own spiritual treasures and cognitively realize the beauty and worth of their own souls. This is the time that they discuss what they need to do when that young mother arrives at the church doorstep with her two children. In this simple structure they become missionaries who see the value and potential worth of their ushering in ways far beyond saying hello to people and handing them a worship bulletin.

Dioceses and regional judicatories have great opportunity to utilize peer engagement at events such as clergy conferences. In addition to having meetings and workshops led by specialist talking heads, clergy can be subdivided into small groups where they share faith stories and talk about what they are doing locally. Each thereby becomes a leader during some moment. This gives each person some responsibility for local vision, methodology, and implementation. Meetings of judicatory leaders can also expand table fellowship to include both faith stories and vision and mission objectives, together with means of implementation. Leaders at any level can learn from what colleagues are doing, gaining insights from shared successes and failures. This feeds souls and enriches participants.

Here are some of the basic components that are typically present when a local church begins to develop a culture of reclaiming Christianity at any level, in any denomination:

Crisis—Something needs "fixing." The crisis needs to be sufficiently obvious that it becomes a forceful motivator to seek examination of causes and a willingness to search for good options. The present crisis is universal Christian decline and the inability to function together in the face of divisive issues.

Base Asset—The fundamental asset of revitalized churches is spirituality, rooted in divine power and guidance. This spirituality has to be explicit and verbalized, not assumed and kept private. Power from on high must be recognized, evidence of it shared, effects of it preached, and results of it celebrated.

Selected Leadership—Church renewal depends on entrepreneurial leadership. Whatever the goal in a church is, those best qualified should be selected to lead. If they succeed, all flourish. The Gathering of Leaders is an invitation-only movement solely because that is the way it can most effectively function as a research and development team. The entire Episcopal Church is healthier in part because of it. When selecting lay table leaders for Christian formation, you will want to choose from those most active, most gifted for the task, and the most entrepreneurial so their faith and skills can not only inaugurate but also refine and further develop the team.

No Rush for Numbers—Jesus began with a few and spent time training. Paul and Barnabas spent a lifetime going from place to place, working in partnership with those they selected. They and their recruits went as small teams and added to their teams wherever they went. Implementation begins with the thorough training of a team. The result is an infrastructure that will endure, effectively creating a new culture that supports new opportunity. Development of infrastructure teams comes first and should never be rushed.

Failures Expected—Some failure is to be expected and is a part of growth. Many stories at Gatherings are about trying something that failed and the helpful learnings that were gleaned.

Failure to try is life-defeating—as documented in the parable of the talents. It's important that clergy and lay leaders have communities of fellow leaders with whom they can share stories of their failures. Because stories of a peer's failed experiment make it clear that churches with no failures are churches that aren't trying anything creative, these stories encourage hearers. It is necessary to try.

Non-hierarchical Peer Learning and Team Development with Spiritual Base—The image of parson/flock, pastor/congregation (or Father knows best) gives way to clergy and laity engaging as peers with a senior pastor (or a designated associate) working more as a player-coach. This unites and empowers staff who are otherwise siloed by function and starved spiritually. And it makes possible an institutional culture that is open, welcoming, expectant, spiritually nurturing, and joyful, with leaders modeling for themselves and the congregation how best to accomplish mission. As coach, the senior pastor gets the final word. Yet in the team setting, there is no hierarchy. Participants contribute on an equal basis, sifting through data, ideas, and possibilities, until time for a final decision, at which time the player-coach exercises the prerogative of making the call.

By way of commentary, in Gatherings this non-hierarchical structure prevails. There are bishops, priests, and a few lay persons. In the mix are those of various positions—those in charge of congregations; staff at congregation, judicatory, seminary, or parochial school levels; educators; campus missioners; chaplains, etc. —all functioning as equal colleagues in pursuit of a common goal. All are quick to relish the feeling of collegiality. It is a very healthy mix.

Personal Self Assessment—In a peer setting, participants know that they will be called upon to reflect on their own ministry or faith experience. Of necessity they make a self-evaluation. Such assessment is a means of growth.

REASONABLE EXPECTATIONS

As always change is slow, but it is likewise sure. The slowness enables the faithful to gradually and nonthreateningly move into a more attractive and nurturing way of being. Little by little people are more open, friendly, expectant, confident, and willing to embrace change. There is no stated numerical growth goal. The first growth has to be in depth and breadth, not numbers. The infrastructure is expanding, and this is the harbinger of numerical growth. The clergy are engaged, happy, productive, confident, fully connected to laity. They relish the deeper spiritual ties with each other and the congregation. Clergy of smaller churches might find themselves very happy to stay where they are, rather than move to a bigger church, because their hopes and aspirations are being met. The divine promises are experienced as their souls are fed even as the souls of the faithful are nurtured. There is no sense of isolation. Instead, the closeness among clergy and laity is precious, highly appreciated, and motivating.

During the process of growth and change, it is good to discuss reasonable expectations for clergy, lay leaders, and members of the congregation. Here are some suggested expectations for you to build upon or adapt, depending on your context.

Focus—When there is a set focus or goal, all work together. The result is positive energy. The goal must be missionary to the core. For instance, the music ministry is not limited to music but considers how music best supports overall mission, including enriching the spiritual base of all who participate.

Nurture—All are nurtured by each other in a peer exchange, spiritually and in creative ideas for the advancement of mission.

Lay Inclusion—Lay participation brings all their acquired skills, professional and otherwise, into visioning and striving for holy goals. Laity are commissioned to make a huge contribution through their developed skills and insights.

Congregational Morale—The enthusiasm, confidence, and development among team members spills over into the larger congregation, greatly strengthening all.

Gospel Transmission—Christianity is caught and then taught when peer engagement is used for Christian formation.

Infrastructure—A new and expanded infrastructure is created with the peer engagement and ministry teams that greatly expands the depth of community, makes no budgetary demands, and adds enormous joy to ministry. This creates a healthy missionary culture.

Results—Spiritual nurture replaces the common assumption that churches automatically provide spiritual support simply because they are churches.

- Mutual respect replaces the common assumption that the church has a monopoly on God.

- Mutual respect gives laity and clergy alike a means to interpret the Holy Scripture by love and to engage and leaven secular culture with scripture's moral guidance, recognizing that any new insight or discovery may raise moral questions.

- Evangelism becomes recruitment with a goal of conversion to a pilgrimage for life through divine power and guidance, with the church being the vehicle where such power and direction is proclaimed, celebrated, and nurtured.

- Christian education is broadened to include divine encounter and the explanation and exploration of those encounters as an enormous source of spiritual nurture.

- Preaching highlights development of spiritual treasure and wealth to equip the faithful for their personal lives and to bless others.

- Music is more lively because there is more connection with the words of hymnody and the singer's spiritual awareness.

- Outreach gains a more spiritual dimension and vigor that comes from the individual's desire to reach outward and beyond.

- Church growth begins by building into a congregation an infrastructure for Christian formation. It is created by loving newcomers, identifying for them their spiritual birthrights, enabling them to nurture their souls, and equipping them to do the same for children and youth.

Congregations equip the faithful for mission beyond the church, and church maintenance is justified for that to occur.

- Clergy adapt to a shared leadership model of ministry through a player-coach model, developing congregations as a ministry team while retaining responsibility for head coach leadership.

- Growth is multidimensional, including spiritual nurture of individuals, infrastructure for mission, vision development and strategy of implementation, and outreach to the hungry of soul, of body, or for social justice.

FINAL THOUGHTS

Clergy yearn inwardly to be united with others in mission, to receive soul-nurture as they minister to others and to lead in the miraculous transformation of lives. Laity yearn for the same—a vibrant and engaging church, one that is equipping the faithful for mission by their growing in spiritual treasure. My prayer is that this book will add to the depth of growth already in progress. The goal is to aid in the creation of a church culture that will make gospel transmission far more effective and Christianity ever more helpful to all, first to the Christian and secondly as a positive witness for good to those beyond. What beauty! We can be buoyed by realizing that efforts underway in various sectors of the Christian world are already leading to recovery, creating a more creative church culture for reclaiming Christianity.

REFLECT AND RESPOND

- What do you see as special or helpful for your ministry or congregation about the vision, mission, core values, and structure of the Gathering of Leaders?

- Why are tweaks to present Christian methodology inadequate for a renewed Christianity?

- What is so powerful about peer engagement?

- What do you think about clergy as team coaches? Is any of this going in your congregation?

- How real is Christian decline for you? What do you think are the root causes of this decline? Are renewal efforts where you serve recognizing and addressing the root causes of decline?

- Do you think spiritual enrichment, and better gospel transmission and mutual respect through love, would attract the growing number of those claiming to be spiritual but not religious?

- If you are a clergy person, how isolated do you feel? If you are a lay person, how isolated do you think your clergy leaders are?

CHAPTER 7
RECLAIMING **GOVERNANCE**

C hurch governance does not, at first blush, appear to be a deeply spiritual topic; many people think words like vestry and canons are inherently tedious. But, in fact, the choices churches make about governance and organization make it more likely that the church will walk down some paths, and less likely that it will walk down others. Decisions about church governance ultimately drive a great deal of churches' mission; directly and indirectly, vestries and canons animate the spirituality of members. Healthy board organization will not, by itself, lead to the reclaiming of Christianity. But it is a tool that should not be overlooked. I developed the model presented here back in the 1970s as rector of St. Mark's Church, Beaumont, Texas, and have been sharing it ever since.

THE STRUCTURE

Church boards—if they are organized appropriately, and if they view themselves appropriately—can be centers of Christian renewal. Conversely, while God will not be thwarted by even the most incompetent vestry, church boards, if organized toxically or if possessed of a distorted self-conception, can do their level best to prevent renewal.

Peer learning and vision are the keys to healthy church governance. The model offered here is for Episcopal Church vestries, which are boards varying in size from six to eighteen members, composed of three subgroups that are elected by congregations for terms of three years. One third of the board rotates each year. Vestries are chaired by the rector, vicar, or priest-in-charge. The rector appoints one of the vestry members to be a senior warden, who, governmentally, is second in command in a congregation and who is in charge in the absence of a rector. (This is the usual structure of selection, though each diocese has its own governing laws, which in some cases can have the senior warden elected by the vestry.) Vestries are in charge of the financial and physical aspects of the congregation and, in consultation with the bishop of its diocese, are authorized to search for and select a new rector when a vacancy occurs. Normally vestries meet monthly.

When they are organized as a committee of the whole, vestry meetings can be deadly and boring. Every member feels compelled to contribute, usually having to pick something to question, taking precious time from others. Any vestry member can make some comment, ask some question or raise some issue in a way that the entire board can become hostage of the least productive participant. Members who have counted it a privilege to serve on the vestry often can't wait until their terms expire when they can pass the "honor" of election to another. Opportunity abounds for something far better and holier.

The model presented here creates shared responsibility, keeps everyone focused on the agenda, engages participants, builds good morale, uses time wisely, gets things done efficiently, and develops leadership. It also provides time for strategic dialogue and gospel reflection. It does all this while keeping meetings to about ninety minutes. In this model, the vestry is divided into three committees: property, administration, and ministry. Everything a church does budget-wise fits easily into one of the three subsections. Each committee has a chair. At the outset of each year, following the election of new vestry members, all place their names on a sheet of paper and list in numerical rank their committee preferences. In many instances, they get their first selection, sometimes their second, and hardly ever their third or least-wanted choice. Hence the vestry already has the advantage of its members working in the areas where they have the most interest.

In forming the vestry organizationally, the rector and senior warden select the committee chairs. In advance of the vestry meeting, they set the agenda for each vestry meeting, using input the senior warden has obtained from the three chairs. Rather than limiting the agenda, this advance work simply means that members need to relay agenda items to their chairs for processing. If the item is for the committee on which the member serves, it is simply processed within the committee and brought to the entire vestry if any action is deemed necessary. These committees meet whenever necessary apart from the entire vestry. For instance, if the roof of the parish house is damaged, it doesn't take the entire vestry to research what needs to be done. Suitable recommendations and initial assessments by the committee begin almost immediately. If vestry approval is needed for repair to begin, a presentation of need and a proposed solution is added to the agenda of the next vestry meeting.

The rector and senior warden meet at a time that is set aside each week. The effect is that this is automatic, easier to cancel or adjust rather than having to schedule it when needed. If either can't make the meeting, they talk by telephone and catch up the next week. This provides a superb time for the two to discuss whatever is happening of importance in the congregation, vestry related or otherwise. When there is no pressing business, it is in part social and in part a time to reflect on the deeper and longer range of challenges that congregations always face.

It is the rector's prerogative in the Episcopal Church to preside at vestry meetings. But a more streamlined way is to delegate the chair to the senior warden. This enables the rector to observe the vestry without having to chair a meeting. It assists the rector because when the warden makes an assignment to a committee chair, the chair is more apt to report back to the warden. This takes the rector out of a loop that is primarily perfunctory. It frees the rector to devote time to strategic and missionary pursuits while simultaneously empowering the senior warden to exercise leadership that in no way requires a seminary education. The senior warden calls the committee chairs before each vestry meeting to see what each wants to place on the agenda, and what action, if any, will require a vote. The vestry agenda is organized on a grid with three vertical columns and three horizontal columns. It looks like this:

In the left vertical column, items the administration committee wants to bring to the whole vestry are delineated by whether the item will require vestry action, whether it is new and needs introduction to the vestry, or whether the item is work underway that necessitates a progress report. If the item is new and requires no action, it is introduced as something that the committee will address. Or, if the item is about a work in progress, it comes under the review line in the diagram. A progress report is then given and a timetable established as to how long the project will take. If the item is for action, after due presentation of the salient material and opportunity for discussion, there is a motion to adopt. Regardless of the status of the items, any vestry member can comment or question. This makes sure no one is bypassed. Each member of the vestry has access to the material developed by the committees as presentations are made. The beauty of this arrangement is that responsibility is shared, and all have a chance to shape the outcome.

Once the business part of the vestry meeting begins, the presider calls upon the committee chairs for reports. If the administration committee goes first and reports and no further action or discussion is needed, another chair is recognized for a similarly structured report. When all three committees have reported, the senior warden is given time for any comments deemed appropriate and then the rector does the same. The rector's comments usually go beyond the scope of the vestry's business and are often focused on major events in the life of the congregation.

A DETAILED DESCRIPTION OF THE FLOW OF THE VESTRY MEETING

The vestry meeting unfolds as follows.

All vestry members gather at a stated hour and place. The meeting begins with worship: a simple opening prayer or some more developed form of worship. Opening prayers are very appropriate, or a group *lectio divina* is sometimes done. While shared prayer is important, keep this brief. Vestry members have opportunity to worship at other times, and thus a longer worship time will take away from the primary vestry mandate of governance.

Immediately following prayer, the three committees meet in separate rooms for twenty minutes. Even though they may have already done their work getting ready for a vestry presentation, the committees gather to reconnect. They can review what they will present. If committee members had not been able to make the most recent committee meeting, they can be brought up to speed. If anything needs updating from the last committee meeting, it can be reported and, if necessary, approved. Hence all committee members enter the vestry meeting completely informed and prepared. Even if there is nothing on the committee's agenda, this meeting is still important. From experience of peer engagement, the bonding of people who share responsibility is a major asset. The committees are team subsets of the vestry team. Team meetings address their assigned tasks, or they can discuss new possibilities. The setting is ripe for building trust. These committee meetings add a community or pastoral dimension to the vestry—the Holy Spirit is often the unseen guest and guide. In the committees, members get to know and appreciate each other in ways that are not possible in a larger group. Vestry members feel they are more successfully exercising the duties for which they were elected. Peer engagement is the operative mode.

The senior warden and rector can visit the committees as they choose. Sometimes the chairs want one or the other, or both, to provide input to their committee. Sometimes non-vestry members who have been invited to the meeting, or who have been given an ex-officio vestry position, are assigned to a committee. For instance, in the congregation I once served, the president of the church women's organization was an ex-officio part of the vestry. Ex-officio officers such as clerks, chancellors, and treasurers can also be included. These meetings also may include staff, most especially clergy staff. These are local options for any vestry.

After twenty minutes, the entire vestry reassembles for its business meeting. The senior warden presides and takes the committee reports one by one. Unless there is an unusually large volume of business, this part of the meeting should be able to conclude within an hour, including the worship, committee meetings, and the meeting of the whole. The process is also streamlined when, by mutual consent, a financial sheet is distributed only quarterly. Elected congregational leaders find it a compelling temptation and even a perceived mandate to review all the figures if they are distributed. Often they can pose questions that can be answered quickly and privately by speaking to the treasurer or committee chair. Hence the recommendation is for a quarterly distribution of the financials, with an update at every meeting on finances and any unusual deviations or problems.

Generally, church budgets are managed well. Often collections run behind revenue, especially during the summer, but experience seems to confirm that there is little a vestry can do that will make a notable change during the course of a year. De-emphasizing the budget, other than a general report by the administration committee on the overall monetary health of the congregation, reclaims otherwise wasted time that can be used more creatively for things more substantive. It should be said parenthetically that monthly budget reports should be made available to any vestry member wanting one. This ensures full transparency and enables the person wanting more information to get it.

Because the budget divides readily into areas covered by each committee, each committee has its own mini-budget. Each year as a proposed budget is developed for the coming year, the committees come up with their respective proposals. These are then given to the administration committee for a preliminary recommendation for the entire anticipated budget. Priorities among committee requests can then be addressed with the rector, senior warden, and the three committee chairs and, ultimately, be presented to the vestry for approval.

Consent calendars can also speed vestry business. Minutes and other written reports can be distributed in advance of the vestry meetings, giving members opportunity to study them and, when appropriate, make suggestions, corrections, or comments. If no cause for change arises, then the consent calendar can be moved and approved, clearing all the more routine material from individual votes. Under this format, any vestry member can ask for an item on the consent calendar to be moved prior to the meeting, returned to its committee of origin, and placed on the regular agenda.

Now to something more creative, strategic, and missional: since an hour and a half is the time people usually allocate as worthy of exercising a responsible board obligation, having a shorter worship/committee meeting/plenary agenda leaves time for topical presentations and discussion. For instance, the vestry can have conversations about Christian formation, stewardship, evangelism, outreach, prayer, or other issues of the day—conversations that will deepen the lives of the vestry participants. These conversations also provide a time of sharing, much like that which occurs during Christian formation classes, which helps bond vestry members to one another. Finally, such substantive conversations add a spiritual element to the meeting time that is greatly fulfilling to members.

When needed, the rector, senior warden, and chairs act as an executive committee. This is usually not necessary, but the structure is there should occasion arise where it would be useful.

ADDITIONAL ASPECTS OF VESTRY CHOREOGRAPHY

Christians, in the tradition of Jesus, need to retreat from time to time, to enter into another kind of space where the press of daily routine and business does not take precedent. Christianity at its core is a fresh, forward-looking, creative, and power-laden movement focused on raising lives heavenward, both for the present and forever. Such a movement needs constant refreshment, time for getting in touch with its deeper roots in Christ and his focus on the transformation of lives and the building of spiritual treasure. A retreat is an opportune time for just such reflection.

Thus, a yearly vestry retreat is enormously beneficial. I advocate scheduling an annual retreat soon after new vestry persons are elected. I recommend that the retreat be held off site and overnight to minimize distractions and optimize community building. Often spouses/partners are included on the retreat. Even in smaller congregations, vestry members may not know others well. Nor will they have served with the same persons toward the same purpose. Retreat time helps constitute the new vestry both as a working group and as a community with shared goals.

At the retreat, no business is conducted beyond the formal organization of the vestry itself. In an overnight setting, the group will have at least two common meals. They can, if the agenda is so shaped, share stories of faith formation. These connect to the very root of spiritual existence and give otherwise hidden insights into others' lives. Nothing is more helpful or precious to a rector or to the individuals who make up the vestry. Furthermore, the kind of vestry organization outlined here depends on trust. Without trust, a vestry's effectiveness will be compromised. Retreats are a crucial step in helping members of a new group learn to trust one another.

Now a word of caution. If the congregation isn't reasonably healthy, implementation of this kind of vestry organization could be premature. My suggestion to those in such places is to address the dysfunction first. Solving the dysfunction is absolutely essential for anything really good to begin happening in a congregation's life. Growth will not occur, bickering will prevail, and little healthy pride will be generated when people don't trust one another. That trust, it should be noted, begins with the rector. Though most often unspoken, the rector's first and foremost job when beginning a new ministry is to establish trust.

THE SATISFACTIONS OF GOOD CHURCH GOVERNANCE

A vestry organized by committees generates high morale. Members may not relish the vestry meeting as the highlight of a week, but it approaches a place of meaningful commitment. The vestry members appreciate its functioning in a truly Christ-like way. They see problems constructively identified and addressed. They grow in their understanding of congregational governance and are able to participate in planning for its longer-term future. Their own spiritual pilgrimage will be deepened as they reflect on gospel priorities in addition to the needs of the church. For a rector, this kind of organization is a jewel. It enables him or her to observe the vestry without being the point person to direct the meeting. It gives insight on the leadership of the chairs, so that it will be easier to pick a senior warden for the next year. Or, if the chair is elected, vestry members can see firsthand how the three chairs function in leadership roles, and this can be an influence on the future election. People feel connected. Rather than each member feeling some obligation to speak in an assembly of the whole, each has an opportunity in committee. Each vestry person feels empowered and has an active part in the life of the vestry.

Of course, there are dysfunctional persons—good and faithful in their intent—who have agendas that counter the otherwise general thrust of the vestry and congregation. For whatever reason, and sometimes even subconsciously, their personal need has the effect of derailing the smooth effectiveness of the whole because of the attention they crave. While such people are most certainly entitled to opinion and position, the committee structure isolates this dysfunction. If the person tries to introduce something not on the agenda, the presider need only refer the concern to an appropriate committee and move on.

There is a maxim that I have found holds true: If a dysfunctional person comes up against a functional system, either that person will convert or leave. Hopefully the dysfunctional one will get on board. But if otherwise, experience dictates that it is far better to let the person go—without feeling any guilt. Otherwise, dysfunction will increase with the undue effort to address the person's personal need. Part of dysfunction is the desire for personal attention. Clergy and laity sometimes assume their job is to please everyone—but that is not good leadership exercised in love.

This isn't a strict blueprint for how every vestry should function. It is an outline. Many vestries have used the general outline and streamlined it for local use. Committee names, timelines, and other procedures can be altered. The central and compelling point is an organizational plan that can not only streamline church board meetings but also help further the church's mission. Since these meetings must be conducted, why not make them the best, most efficient, most mission-focused and mutually respectful of all persons that they can be?

The Rev. Canon Andrea McMillin (administrative assistant to the bishop of Northern California) reports that this model of vestry leadership brings both improved efficiency and increased leadership to a congregation. She says, "This model enabled us to call more people into leadership. Some of our church members had been reluctant to serve on the vestry, as the meetings were too lengthy and unfocused. By narrowing our purpose, making prayer a priority, and pushing work out into committees, we opened up leadership opportunities within the vestry as well as other areas."

FINAL THOUGHTS

What has been presented in this model is primarily for carrying out the vestry's fiduciary responsibility. But vestries are also about mission and vision. Bob Schorr, retired from the corporate world and as of this writing on the staff of the Episcopal Diocese of Texas, includes a more mission-oriented reflection on governance that can help clergy and vestries live into their gospel calling. Drawing from Richard Chait, William Ryan, and Barbara Taylor's book, *Governance as Leadership, Reframing the Work of Nonprofit Boards*, Schorr discusses the work of governance utilizing three categories or approaches: fiduciary, strategic, and generative. Each is important and necessary and has its appropriate time and purpose. The fiduciary has been discussed already.

The strategic mode includes development, articulation, and implementation of congregational goals. It involves longer-term planning, review of the community setting, assessment of community needs, and evaluation of resources within the congregation to minister to those in the congregation and to engage and serve the community beyond the lot line. Consider a paraphrase from the late Bishop William Temple: The church is the only entity in society that exists for the benefit of those who are not its members. Thus good governance and mission must move beyond the temporal affairs of the buildings and congregation and into the Great Commission and the second part of the Great Commandment, to love our neighbors as ourselves—and to be the hands and feet of Christ in our community.

The generative mode occurs at an even higher elevation. When the text "Glory to God whose power working within us is able to accomplish abundantly far more than all we can ask or imagine" (Ephesians 3:20) is considered, there is license to dream. This is the creative space for governance where intellectual playfulness can unlock new ideas and uncover new perspectives. It is the space for rich and animated discourse, but without an urgency to decide, check off a box, and move on to the next thing.

Once, years ago when I was the rector of a church, the vestry and I chartered a bus to drive us to our retreat, which was some two-and-a-half hours from our church. During the trip, I asked the vestry to speculate on how they would spend $10 million should such a sum be put at our disposal, with the provision that all of it be spent within two years. It caused some bit of stir in a very good way, breaking us out of self-imposed limitation and enabling us to think beyond usual boundaries. This is generative. It participates in God's abundance. And it ties all of us to our higher identity.

REFLECT AND RESPOND

+ How effective is your vestry or governing board in its organization and structure?

+ How would the members of your board adapt to the structure presented here? What would be the challenges of implementing this structure? What would be the fruits?

+ To what degree does the board of your church address strategic and generative responsibilities?

+ How does the model here promote leadership development and utilization of leadership talent of those on its board?

+ How would you rate the morale level of your church's governing board? Why?

CHAPTER 8

RECLAIMING **YOUTH FOR LEADERSHIP**

W hen I was a teenager, I had a special interest in church. I was moved by the worship, especially the singing. I was strongly drawn to our rector. He was well-known in our town of 25,000. An amazing accomplishment during his thirty-eight-year tenure as rector of the Episcopal Church of the Heavenly Rest in Abilene, Texas, was the congregation's building a magnificent, true Gothic church, designed by the same architect who did the Episcopal National Cathedral in Washington, D.C. As spectacular as that was, the rector was best known for giving away his coats in wintertime during the depression years of the 1930s. He would give them to others, remembering he could go to an office or home that would be warm. Among his other fine attributes was the keen interest he took in the youth of the church. This was affirming to all of us because, in the adult world, we children and youth were often invisible—not just out of sight but utterly out of consideration. But Parson, as we called him, saw the people we were and the people we were becoming, and he wanted to help us in that becoming.

I've already told the story of delivering flowers to shut-ins after Christmas and Easter services. Parson sent me as a teenager on what could be called errands of assistance. One involved Speedy Watkins (not his real name), once a star high school athlete who as an adult became a drug addict. While he recovered from the addiction, he was left with a kind of palsy that severely limited his ability to function. He could do yard work but little more. He lived in a hotel that barely met any standard of acceptability. Parson would on occasion get clothes for him, and I delivered them. Through such errands of mercy, and by serving as an acolyte for funerals and weddings as well as for Sunday worship, I learned a great deal about ministry, its vision, its power, its effect beyond worship and education, and its enormous joys.

While Parson wanted me to prepare for ordination, I, at first, chose another path. It took twelve years beyond high school graduation for me to come to see what he had long seen in me—that I, like everyone, had a divine calling. My calling included a good college education at Rice University, a period of working as a chemical engineer, and participation at Trinity Church, Victoria, Texas, as a young adult. It included marriage to Barbara, a high school classmate. And, eventually, it included seminary and ordination.

The point of this story is the need and opportunity for pastors and lay leaders to intentionally mentor young people and help them develop as Christian leaders. I was mentored in ministry as a teenager, and that mentoring would have served me and the church well for a lifetime, even if I had not been called to ordination. I learned the academics of ministry in seminary, but I learned the heart of it—the beauty and power of it—by being mentored by Parson during my teenage years.

All baptized Christians have a ministry, and clergy have an obligation to call teenagers into ministry, either lay or ordained. Seeds can be sown; some will sprout immediately and others will sprout years later. I sowed such a seed in my first year as a rector at St. Mark's Church, Beaumont, Texas. The women of St. Mark's gave me some money to do "whatever you think would aid in the church's mission." I hired John Lewis and John Newton, graduating seniors, to do community ministry during the summer, running errands and completing small chores for people with special needs as well as working in community agencies. At the end of the summer, I challenged both of these seniors to think about the ordained ministry as a life's calling.

They thanked me. What I didn't know at the time was that once they were alone, they laughed heartily at the very thought of considering the priesthood. Both went on to law school and became very good attorneys. John Lewis, however, grew more and more restless within his profession, finally realizing that he indeed had a call to Holy Orders. This led him recently to send me a gift he had bought while visiting the Holy Land. He included a note saying, "I think about you often and wish I had followed your direction to go to seminary instead of law school. I am so excited about my work as a priest." He had found and still finds a deep joy as a missionary. His witness to the faith has brought joy to me, and through him, to many others. His story reveals how the divine works always and everywhere in ways beyond human detection.

I asked John to reflect upon his early years of Christian experience to highlight the opportunity the church of today has for the nurturing the young. He writes:

> I don't think my Sunday School education at St. Mark's helped me recognize and understand the crucial

contrast between the standards for living discipleship in the kingdom of God and following the standards of the world. By the time I worked for you that summer, I was already firmly committed on seeking "success" through a life in the legal profession. If in those early years I was taught the spiritual discipline of prayerful discernment, I don't remember it. And even though I learned a lot of Bible stories, I did not come away with an understanding about how these stories might shape my daily living and character formation. Also back then at home we never read the Bible or talked about how the life of Jesus ought to shape our daily lives. I think that was supposed to take place mostly through osmosis. That did not prove to be effective in my case.

Nevertheless, the foundation that was laid for me at St. Mark's later saved me. After a few years of complete dedication in law practice, I woke up one day and realized that my life was a mess. Even though I had achieved everything I set to accomplish both professionally and financially—and then some—I was miserable. Success and self-sufficiency did not deliver the happiness or satisfaction I always heard and believed they would. For the first time in my life, I realized that I did not have all the answers or the power to make my own life meaningful. At that point, the only place I knew to turn was to God and the church.

Now a priest, John Lewis founded the Saint Benedict's Workshop in San Antonio, Texas, with a mission for "equipping individuals and communities to use the Bible in practices of discernment and discipleship in all areas of daily life as they are transformed over time into the image of Christ." He is a part-time associate rector at St. Mark's, San Antonio. In 2016 he entered into a contract with the Seminary of the Southwest to serve as director of their formational outreach, which includes the Iona Collaborative that trains non-stipendiary clergy for a number of Episcopal dioceses.

Although his work is more focused on those preparing for ordination, there is a distinct parallel with *Reclaiming Christianity* in John's insistence that formation is foundational. He writes, "Over time I have grown ever more confident that Christian formation lies at the heart of Christianity. My hope is that more congregations will introduce the practices of spiritual discernment to their members, especially to younger Christians." Parenthetically, the other John who did summer ministry as a youth with John Lewis—John Newton—became an attorney and his son has become a priest, the Rev. Canon John Newton IV, formerly chief of staff for the Diocese of Texas and more recently rector of St. Michael's Church, Austin.

Earlier in this book I mentioned the Rev. Jimmy Bartz. Like John Lewis, he too is one I challenged to consider ordained ministry as a life's calling while I was rector of St. Martin's in Houston. Unlike John Lewis, Jimmy's response was more immediate. After becoming a bishop, I had the joy of seeing him transition from college to seminary, and the added joy of seeing his priestly work blossom everywhere he has served.

Still, at the congregational level, I see little evidence of grooming youth for lay or ordained ministry. One reason for this is that clergy have so much to do simply to keep their churches viable. With a weakened spirituality and means of spiritual transformation, crippled by conflict within congregations and among denominations, and besieged by a rising secularization of culture, clergy have little time to devote to the training of the young for ministry. Youth are not invited to consider ordained ministry as a viable option. Perhaps clergy might think, "What bright young person would envision a fulfilling life's work as a member of the clergy in the midst of such church decline?" Yet as clergy (and lay leaders), one of our central roles is to help others as they discern God's call for their lives. For some youth, that might take shape by challenging them to listen and discern whether they have a call to ordained ministry.

This reluctance to train must change—and will as Christianity is reclaimed. The obvious first step is the recovery of health for the church, to which the thrust of this book is directed. But it is not too early to begin visioning the possibilities of what should take center stage in the life of a renewed church, a reclaimed Christianity. Christian formation, around which the future church will revolve, is most certainly within the scope of congregations as they transition to a new model of ministry. Just as Christianity is caught and then taught to adults, isn't the same true for youth as well?

The Rev. Morgan Allen, rector of the Episcopal Church of the Good Shepherd, Austin, Texas, says, "I can imagine a program between one's junior and senior years in high school. This might need to be rooted in a parochial context where the teenagers' curiosity could be raised in an environment for meaningful expression, all with a peer community wherein reflective conversations could be shared." This approach would encourage participants to talk with others about their thoughts about vocation—any vocation. Teens might be talking about pastry baking and lawyering and social work, but since the setting would be at church, it would be natural to introduce ordained ministry into the mix. Clergy could talk about the joys and strains of their callings, and they could speak with teens about God's call to challenge all to accept their spiritual birthrights, develop their souls, and offer themselves for the building of a holier, just, merciful, and compassionate society.

One such initiative was launched some years ago at the Episcopal Church of St. Michael and All Angels, Dallas, Texas, called Pathways to Ministry. The church secured sufficient funding to inaugurate a ministry to high school students centered on opportunities and challenges of Christian leadership, whether ordained or lay. The ministry also included a summer intern program for college students. The Rev. Claire Makins, curate at the Church of the Heavenly Rest, Abilene, served for six weeks in Pathways in 2000 while she was an undergraduate student at the University of the South. "The parishioners were excited we were there," she writes. "Lay people volunteered to be on a discernment committee for us, and we met throughout our time to discuss how we were feeling about a possible call. We had weekly meetings with the rector. My experience gave me first-hand insight into what priests do on a day-to-day basis. Scary as it was, it helped me to say 'yes' to the call."

Still another part of this same ministry was an intern arrangement where college graduates spent a year in the congregation. They worked in the community with various kinds of outreach ministries and as a team interfaced with each other and clergy at church in both academic discovery of Christian heritage and sharing their experiences in the mission field. This three-tiered ministry for high schoolers, college students, and college graduates was quite dynamic but unfortunately did not continue once its grant funding expired.

Another example of such a ministry comes from the Episcopal Church of St. John the Divine in Houston, Texas. It had a quite extensive fellowship ministry in the early 2000s for college graduates seeking training and experience with Christian leadership. Six to eight fellowships were offered annually. Those enrolled were housed in homes of parishioners, which included some meals as well. The fellows were given part-time jobs in the social and ministry agencies in the Houston area, from which they drew a modest stipend for working three days a week. The other weekdays were spent at the church in peer engagement and study. This was led by a lay person, Meg Rice, under supervision of the then rector, the Rev. Laurens Hall. Staff clergy and laity led courses in theology, Bible, church history, and more. Sharing of ministry experience bonded the participants together in deeper ways and greatly enhanced the spiritual lives of participants. Magnificent and deep relationships formed between the fellows and their host families.

In the 1980s, various grassroots programs devoted to the vision of young adults living in community, serving their neighborhoods, sharing faith formation, and discerning vocational direction began to be developed in the Episcopal Church. Since 2009 these initiatives have come together as the Episcopal Service Corps. The Corps's constitutive programs number more than twenty as of 2018 with corps members in the field in various cities across the United States. Their stated vision is "Following Jesus as intentional communities of service, justice, and prayer."

These models have tremendous potential. It would seem a natural next step, as churches become centers of a renewed Christianity, for congregations to develop their own versions of such programs. With a bold vision and a growing, highly committed, and confident congregation, such initiatives would not have to wait on grant money to get started. Once laity grow to be more fully involved in leading ministry, they can use skills already honed through their secular expertise to vision, plan, and initiate ministries with teens, college students, and young adults. Devoting time, energy, thought, prayer, and creativity into equipping the young with spiritual skills is an important way for churches to live into a reclaimed faith. Such ministries also keep older adults engaged with the transmission of faith, and it would allow young people to consider a deeper level of Christian leadership.

FINAL THOUGHTS

Opportunity knocks. We may be in a moment of institutional church decline, but the map for the future is becoming clearer. Realizing that faith is caught and then taught enables churches to move into a Christian formation model that nurtures the soul, every human's birthright. Commitment to the team as the basic Christian building block recovers for our time a historic Christian leadership model. Emancipating scripture through interpretation by love will allow scripture to once again be a guide through, rather than an antagonist in, battles about cultural change.

REFLECT AND RESPOND

- What attention is given in your congregation to equipping youth for Christian leadership and possible ordination?

- Is peer engagement any part of Christian formation for youth in your congregation, and if so, what role does it play? If it is not a practice, what possibilities does it offer?

- Are youth in your congregation equipped to read scripture through the lens of love?

- How can you engage with the youth of your congregation? What can you teach them? What can they teach you?

AFTERWORD

This book is rooted in my own spiritual journey from adolescence to present—a journey to understand the reasons for church decline and to ascertain ways to reverse it. It is a story of growth, through countless challenges, many of which changed my basic outlook. I've had much to learn and am still in that process. With changes occurring faster than many of us can fully comprehend, there is occasion for all who care deeply about the health and future of the church to become a team of explorers, giving thanks as good things happen, and using disappointment as a means of deeper insight. In my opinion, this is the process for the reclaiming of Christianity. The spiritual treasure and its source are there—in each of our churches and in all the baptized. Spiritual hunger abounds, and souls await being fed more fully.

May God bless each of you as you join the present challenge to build a society much in need of what is holy.

ACKNOWLEDGMENTS

I want to express appreciation to the countless number of those who have encouraged, mentored, affirmed and empowered me throughout my life: friends, teachers, extended family members and colleagues, from childhood onward.

I am grateful for my professors at Rice University and the Church Divinity School of the Pacific; my mentors at Union Carbide (now Dow Chemical); bishops and fellow clergy and lay leaders, especially in the Diocese of Texas and Carol Barnwell in particular; parishioners at Epiphany, Kingsville, St. Mark's, Houston, St. Mark's, Beaumont, and St. Martin's, Houston, where I served, and all the faithful of the dioceses of Texas and West Texas; colleagues in the Anglican Communion Compass Rose Society; colleagues in the Gathering of Leaders, especially John Castle; my deceased family members and godparents from childhood in Abilene; Parson Willis Gerhart who taught me ministry and Bishop Scott Field Bailey who guided my priesthood; parishioners at present and deceased at the Church of the Heavenly Rest, Abilene, where I grew up and where I have now returned; and my children and grandchild.

Finally, and far more significant, I dedicate this book to my wife, my life's partner, an integral part of my inner self, my constant support, and my deepest love. In her own way, she very much a part of this book. To her and as witness to my readers, I say:

Because I have you, each day grows richer,
Because I have you, I am more secure.
Because I have you, my life glows brighter,
Because I have you, I always endure.

Because I have you, I am never lonely,
Even when away, you are in my heart.
Because I have you, I know that you only
Are that of which I am always a part.

Because I have you, I am the stronger,
Because I have you, my worries are less.
Because I have you, my view is longer,
Because I have you, it's easier to bless.

Because you are there, life is much fuller,
Because you are there, my life is enhanced.
Because you are there, burdens are lesser,
Because you are there, my soul is advanced.

Because you are there, I strive all the more,
Because you are there, I want you to know,
My aim is to please, and I seek to adore.
Because you are there, my heart is aglow.

Because I have you, years have more meaning,
Because I have you, I know your support.
Because I have you, each day is redeeming,
Because I have you, my ship has a port.

Because I have you, death cannot conquer,
Because I have you, your presence endures.
Because I have you, I will never falter,
Your presence within my wellness ensures.

ABOUT **THE AUTHOR**

C laude E. Payne's strategic and analytic insights for vision and change management come from his chemical engineering training and work afterward in the chemical industry. He applied this approach to ministry, first as a campus missioner and subsequently in leading congregations. After twenty-five years serving two large Episcopal churches, he was elected to bishop in the Episcopal Diocese of Texas, which grew in number during his episcopate. He documented the story of this growth in *Reclaiming the Great Commission*, a bestselling book that he coauthored with Hamilton Beazley. Continuing ministry in retirement, Claude co-founded The Gathering of Leaders. This movement has attracted more than 500 bishops and clergy in the Episcopal Church and Anglican Church of Canada and developed into a research and development team to further mission. He holds three honorary doctorate degrees. In 1996 he was named a distinguished alumnus of Rice University. He is married with two children.

ABOUT **FORWARD MOVEMENT**

Forward Movement is committed to inspiring disciples and empowering evangelists. Our ministry is lived out by creating resources such as books, small-group studies, apps, and conferences. Our daily devotional, *Forward Day by Day*, is also available in Spanish (*Adelante Día a Día*) and Braille, online, as a podcast, and as an app for smartphones or tablets.

It is mailed to more than fifty countries, and we donate nearly 30,000 copies each quarter to prisons, hospitals, and nursing homes. We actively seek partners across the church and look for ways to provide resources that inspire and challenge. A ministry of the Episcopal Church for more than eighty years, Forward Movement is a nonprofit organization funded by sales of resources and by gifts from generous donors.

To learn more about Forward Movement and our resources, visit www.ForwardMovement.org. We are delighted to be doing this work and invite your prayers and support.